Help Students Improve Their Study Skills

Also available:

Assisting Learning and Supporting Teaching
A Practical Guide for the Teaching Assistant in the Classroom
Anne Watkinson
1-85346-794-4

The Essential Guide for Competent Teaching Assistants
Meeting the National Occupational Standards at Level 2
1-84312-008-9

The Essential Guide for Experienced Teaching Assistants
Meeting the National Occupational Standards at Level 3
Anne Watkinson
1-84312-009-7

Professional Values and Practice
The Essential Guide for Higher Level Teaching Assistants
Anne Watkinson
1-84312-250-2

Learning and Teaching
The Essential Guide for Higher Level Teaching Assistants
Anne Watkinson
1-84312-251-0

Supporting Literacy and Numeracy
A Guide for Teaching Assistants
Glenys Fox and Marian Halliwell
1-85346-679-4

Teaching Assistants
Practical Strategies for Effective Classroom Support
Maggie Balshaw and Peter Farrell
1-85346-828-2

A Handbook for Learning Support Assistants
Teachers and Assistants Working Together
Revised Edition
Glenys Fox
1-84312-081-X

Help Students Improve Their Study Skills

A Handbook for Teaching Assistants in Secondary Schools

Jane Dupree

 David Fulton Publishers

David Fulton Publishers Ltd
The Chiswick Centre, 414 Chiswick High Road, London W4 5TF

www.fultonpublishers.co.uk
www.onestopeducation.co.uk

First published in Great Britain by David Fulton Publishers
Reprinted 2006

10   9   8   7   6   5   4   3   2

David Fulton Publishers is a division of Granada Learning Limited,
part of ITV plc.

British Library Cataloguing in Publication Data
A catalogue record for this book is available from the British Library.

ISBN 1 84312 263 4

Typeset by Servis Filmsetting Ltd, Manchester

Contents

Dedication

This book is dedicated to all of the students I have taught, who over the years have allowed me to share in the way they learn and trusted in me enough to try the skills I have shared. It is also dedicated to my husband Graham, who encouraged me to spend the time writing so that others could share these skills, when he knows my real pleasure is in working with students, teachers and teaching assistants 'at the coalface'.

Preface

This book stems from the author's work with students of all abilities who, over several years, have shared their learning styles, difficulties and triumphs and encouraged the author to trial a collection of practical methods to improve study skills, together with explaining to students some theoretical understanding of why they work. It is primarily written for teaching assistants working in mainstream classrooms who form an important bridge between students and teachers. Teaching assistants come to this rewarding job from a variety of backgrounds and with a variety of experience. They are keen to develop skills to make themselves a more effective support mechanism for students.

The book allows chapters to be read in any order, and there is cross-referencing as the need arises. It offers practical solutions to study skills using examples from across the curriculum, both at Key Stage 3 and Key Stage 4.

Many terms given in *italic* in the text can be found in the glossary.

The book is primarily aimed at teaching assistants, but parents and mentors running out-of-school study clubs may also benefit from it.

Teaching and learning styles

Chapter overview

How often have you had to think quickly on your feet, adapting and explaining the lesson task so that the students you are supporting understand and engage with their work? Humans absorb information about their surroundings using a variety of senses. These are related to types of learning styles and the way we prefer to think. Successful students recognise which styles suit them and can adapt tasks accordingly. Educationalists describe these learning differences and preferences using a variety of terms, and these will be introduced in this chapter. However, to support you in adapting tasks, the following three learning styles will be discussed in detail: auditory learners; visual learners; and kinaesthetic learners. By the end of this chapter you will be able to:

- recognise the three main learning styles;
- identify your own and students' preferred styles;
- have practical examples of how to adapt learning tasks to suit different students; and
- understand why students react and think differently.

Introduction

Working within a secondary school environment will have made you aware that there is currently much interest in adapting and delivering lessons so that more students are able to take an active part and therefore be successful learners. If you are a teaching assistant who has supported Maths and English lessons you will be aware of the changes in the curriculum at Key Stage 3 and the way these lessons are delivered. You may have noticed 'mini' whiteboards being used by all students, or the use of an interactive whiteboard. However, many schools have always used a variety of ways to support students with their learning across the curriculum. Modern Languages departments often use role-play; Humanities departments use debates and mock elections to engage learners; Science departments use investigation and experiments; while Geography departments take students on field trips, to name a few. All of these are examples of different teaching styles. What you will have also noticed is the different ways students react to them. Some students are really excited by being allowed to role-play and will remember the content of that lesson well when asked to recall it. Some will have appeared to enjoy the lesson but gained little understanding from it and others will have shown their displeasure at having to role-play and will have asked to do work in their exercise book instead. This is because we all have different preferred learning styles. Some students can adapt their learning styles easily and learn in a variety of ways; others are less flexible and can only learn when material is presented to them in their preferred learning style. Matching the lesson to everyone in the class is a tall order for any teacher. However, if students know their own preferred learning style, they can adapt what they have been asked to do to maximise their learning. As a teaching assistant you are in a unique position. You can work with small groups and observe individuals. This will allow you to identify students' learning styles and help adapt the task. Ultimately your goal is to support them in understanding their own learning style and becoming independent learners, the emotional aspects of which will be returned to in Chapter 2.

Learning styles

What are learning styles? The three main styles that are discussed are: *auditory learners*; *visual learners*; and *kinaesthetic learners* (sometimes known as learning by doing or 'motor' learners). You will often see this referred to as VAK learning (Visual, Auditory and Kinaesthetic).

Auditory learners

As the term suggests auditory learners like to take in information by 'listening'. (This can be information read out loud or their own 'voice' as they read, heard internally.) This is partly because they are good at dealing with language. They like words and have a high understanding of them and their meanings. Additionally, they find it easy to express themselves, by talking to you, their teacher or friends about their learning. Auditory learners:

■ are comfortable in classrooms where there is a high level of teacher talk;

- will remember and follow instructions given by teachers verbally;
- are more likely to put their hand up to answer a question;
- are happy when dealing with large amounts of writing in textbooks;
- retain interesting facts and discussions they have heard on the radio or in conversation;
- recall new ideas and words that have been introduced verbally or written as words on the board during the lesson;
- express themselves well through written work;
- revise successfully by reading and re-reading their notes and textbooks;
- revise successfully using keyword cards;
- will not find mind mapping or concept mapping helpful;
- will read through the instructions of a game or assembly kit before assembling it.

Visual learners

Again, this learning style explains itself; visual learners prefer to 'see' things. This can be literally, i.e. they will look at the pictures or diagrams in a textbook to learn something before they turn to the text. Mentally, they prefer to make pictures in their head and visualise information as a whole. For example, visual learners are often extremely good at being able to rotate 3D pictures in their mind's eye and imagine the new perspective, something that a student with a strong auditory preference would find difficult and a definite asset in today's visual and computer-literate society. As a teaching assistant it is important that you start to recognise the visual learners in the classroom. Since they learn best by visualising the 'end-product', they will not be comfortable, or ready to grapple, with a task in small, sequenced steps unless they know where they are heading. You will recognise these students; they often ask, 'Why are we doing this?' Effective support means explaining the end before the start!

Visual learners:

- are comfortable in lessons that present information colourfully, using pictures, tables, charts, diagrams and videos;
- learn quickly from pictures and diagrams;
- can be mislead by poorly chosen textbooks or worksheets where the pictures do not illustrate the text well. For visual learners, it is *vital* that any pictures or diagrams are well chosen for their quality of content and not just because they look 'pretty' or break up the text;

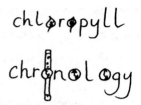

Figure 1.1 *Learning key words using visual clues*

■ are uncomfortable with large amounts of unbroken text;

■ will lose concentration when there is a high level of 'talk' in the learning task;

■ like to know the end point of a task before starting;

■ respond well to a variety of colours and change of shape when learning key words and new vocabulary in lessons, as in Figure 1.1;

■ will find mind mapping and concept mapping helpful (see Chapter 5);

■ will use diagrams to assemble kits and choose recipes etc. that have clear pictures.

Kinaesthetic learners

Kinaesthetic literally means 'touch' or 'feel'. Therefore kinaesthetic learners are those whose preferred learning style is 'hands on'. They learn best when they are allowed to move around and *do* things as part of the learning process. Once they have experienced the learning in a practical way it will be retained well (see Chapter 5). However, they may have difficulty explaining in words what they know. It is easy to see why students whose preferred learning style is strongly kinaesthetic may be disadvantaged in many lessons. Additionally, as a teaching assistant you can begin to see why arguments in some lessons may emerge. For example, if when students are divided into groups to conduct a science experiment the group contains all strongly kinaesthetic learners, there is going to be a battle, as they will all want to *do* (pouring, mixing, measuring, assembling) and no-one will want to record the results. They need an auditory learner in the group for this purpose.

Kinaesthetic learners:

■ learn through doing, then reading and writing, not the other way around (don't expect them to write up the experiment heading, equipment or draw the diagram before they start; let them do it afterwards but insist it is done);

- may fidget in class, including doodling and pen chewing to help their thinking, so provide a doodle pad and don't lend out your pencil (insisting they keep still may not be the best way to help them learn);
- are comfortable in practical areas of the curriculum such as design technology, science, PE, art and ICT;
- may lose concentration and build resentment in these subjects when they are given theory before practice;
- think creatively when planning and designing;
- give poor verbal explanations unless they can touch, draw, make gestures or point while explaining;
- may 'shrug' as a response to a question if they do not have the verbal skills to explain themselves;
- need to find revision methods that link movement with memory; for example, listening to revision notes on a mini disc or 'ipod' whilst running; going for a walk; remembering which classroom they were in and what they were doing when they learnt a skill; writing out key words over and over to transfer them from their 'motor' memory to their long-term memory (see Chapter 5);
- will throw away the written instructions and diagrams in a game or kit and start to assemble it straight away.

Recognising students' learning styles

Learning styles can be recognised in three ways:

- through observation;
- through specially designed questionnaires;
- by watching a student's eye movements as they recall or think about something, using Neuro Linguistic Programming (NLP) techniques.

Observation

Having read some of the bullet points above you will, by now, have started to recognise some of the learning styles of the students that you work with. Observation really is the best way of identifying a student's learning strengths. Remember that many students will be comfortable using a variety of learning styles. It is those students whose preferred style is very rigid who will need most support in recognising this and adapting their study methods. Below are some useful observation strategies that will help you.

1. In whose lessons is the student most happy and successful? It is often because the student's preferred style exactly mirrors their teacher's. What does this teacher's lesson 'look like'? How are these lessons introduced? How does this teacher assess the student's learning?

2. Listen to the language the student uses. Often metaphors match their preferred learning style. 'I **see** what you mean' and 'Try to **see** things my way' are sayings likely to be used by a visual learner; whereas 'I've got a **feel** for it now' is clearly a kinaesthetic learner. There is a list of often-used metaphors (Appendix 1.1 – VAK metaphors) to photocopy and refer to at the end of this book.

3. When given a textbook, where does the student look first? Do they dive straight into the text, or do they look at the pictures?

4. When they recall something successfully as part of a lesson or topic, you should review how that part of the learning was taught originally?

Learning style questionnaires

There are several questionnaires that can be given to adults and children to determine preferred learning styles. If you use the internet and go to any search engine, such as Google, and type in the key words learning + style + questionnaire, you will find plenty to choose from. Some of them are free and many are completed and marked for you on line. Also students really enjoy completing them, so they are a useful lunchtime, study club or breakfast club activity. Before you answer them, write down what preferred style or styles you think you use, based on what you have read so far. If you wish to know more about using ICT, including the internet, refer to *ICT for Teaching Assistants* by John Galloway (David Fulton Publishers; ISBN: 1 84312 203 0).

Observing eye movements

Using an idea from Neuro-Linguistic Programming (which studies behaviours that make people successful and then tries to teach these to others) you can look at a student's eye movements to see their preferred learning style. Briefly, if the student's eyes move upwards they are visual, if they move downwards they are kinaesthetic, and if they move to the side they are auditory. This simple technique is reasonably accurate. Next time you watch a student thinking about an answer or recalling a difficult spelling, watch where his/her eyes go. You will see in Figure 1.2 a student using a kinaesthetic method for their times tables. Note the eye position.

Figure 1.2 *Using the kinaesthetic method*

Applying learning styles in the classroom

As you read through the chapters within this book you will note that the practical suggestions use as many different learning styles as possible. This will allow you to select and use the ideas to suit the students you work with. Within this chapter we will look at one extreme example of how differing learning styles affect students' learning.

Learning the times tables

Did you learn the times tables easily and naturally? Do you dread a student asking you a times table question? Learning the times tables is most often taught using auditory learning. Each table is repeated, rather like a poem, until students can recall the answers instantly. Auditory learning is the quickest and most efficient way of learning the times tables and should be attempted by all. However, as we have noted, not everyone is an auditory learner and many students arrive at secondary school unable to recall their tables, despite the fact that they have been taught well and understand the mathematics of tables. So how can the times tables be learnt using visual or kinaesthetic methods? Most students who do not know their tables are bought an audio-tape to help them learn. It is usually unsuccessful as it is just a different method of auditory learning.

Visual learning

Many students have used a times table square, but not to show them visually how much they already know. In addition, completing the times table square visually is useful for students who have additional time in their maths exam. It can be made and referred to for multiplication, division, square numbers, square roots etc. A template blank square is available for photocopying in Appendix 1.2.

The times table is completed in the order shown below. You will see that as the table is filled in, students can see that they already know lots of it.

Order of completion:

1 × table, across then down

10 × table, across then down

5 × table, across then down

9 × table, across using the method as shown, i.e. starting with the 9 digit, go down the table writing 8,7,6,5,4,3,2,1 until you reach the 0 and then from the bottom of the 9 × table line, go back up, starting with the 9 and decreasing the numbers 9,8,7,6,5,4,3,2,1.

2 × table across then down

You will see how small the squares of missing tables now are. All of this so far can be completed extremely quickly.

1	2	3	4	5	6	7	8	9	10
				1 × table					

1	2	3	4	5	6	7	8	9	10
2									
3									
4									
5				1 × table					
6									
7									
8									
9									
10									

1	2	3	4	5	6	7	8	9	10
2									20
3									30
4									40
5				+ 10 × table					50
6									60
7									70
8									80
9									90
10	20	30	40	50	60	70	80	90	100

1	2	3	4	5	6	7	8	9	10
2				10					20
3				15	5 × table				30
4				20					40
5	10	15	20	25	30	35	40	45	50
6				30					60
7				35					70
8				40					80
9				45					90
10	20	30	40	50	60	70	80	90	100

Figure 1.3

9 × table method ↓ 　　　9 × table method

1	2	3	4	5	6	7	8	9	10
2				10				8	20
3				15				7	30
4				20				6	40
5	10	15	20	25	30	35	40	45	50
6				30				4	60
7				35				3	70
8				40				2	80
9				45				1	90
10	20	30	40	50	60	70	80	90	100

1	2	3	4	5	6	7	8	9	10
2				10				18	20
3				15				27	30
4				20				36	40
5	10	15	20	25	30	35	40	45	50
6				30				54	60
7				35				63	70
8				40				72	80
9				45				81	90
10	20	30	40	50	60	70	80	90	100

↑

1	2	3	4	5	6	7	8	9	10
2	4	6	8	10	12	14	16	18	20
3	6			15				27	30
4	8			20				36	40
5	10	15	20	25	30	35	40	45	50
6	12			30				54	60
7	14			35				63	70
8	16			40				72	80
9	18	27	36	45	54	63	72	81	90
10	20	30	40	50	60	70	80	90	100

Figure 1.4

The student then continues to complete the table in the suggested order: 3s, 4s, 6s, 7s and, finally, 8s (adding on for each number if necessary). By the time they complete the 8 × table there is only one square to fill in, (8x8). A completed table is shown on the next page.

It also has the square roots shown as they can be seen in a diagonal. One student I worked with, who was excellent at maths but as a strongly visual learner did not know her times tables, also pointed out that the end digits in the square root table are the same, coming from the outside of the table top and bottom to the centre. I would not have seen this.

Kinaesthetic learning

You may be familiar with the finger method used to teach the nine times table. This is kinaesthetic learning. However, there is a finger method that you can use to work out all of the tables from the 6× table and above. Since most students already know the lower and easier

$\sqrt{1}$	2	3	4	5	6	7	8	9	10
2	$\sqrt{4}$	6	8	10	12	14	16	18	20
3	6	$\sqrt{9}$	12	15	18	21	24	27	30
4	8	12	$\sqrt{16}$	20	24	28	32	36	40
5	10	15	20	$\sqrt{25}$	30	35	40	45	50
6	12	18	24	30	$\sqrt{36}$	42	48	54	60
7	14	21	28	35	42	$\sqrt{49}$	56	63	70
8	16	24	32	40	48	56	$\sqrt{64}$	72	80
9	18	27	36	45	54	63	72	$\sqrt{81}$	90
10	20	30	40	50	60	70	80	90	$\sqrt{100}$

Suggested order: ×1, ×10, ×5, ×9 (produced visually), ×2, ×3, ×4, ×6, ×7, ×8
Time taken:
Error rate:

Figure 1.5 *Visually learning the times table*

ones, there is an incentive to learn this method for the higher ones (especially for use in mental arithmetic). Known sometimes as the Romany Method, as it is often attributed to being first used by the Romany culture, it is explained below. When teaching in a prison, I watched an inmate use the method while completing his GCSE. (Being a burglar, I am sure you would agree that he was a kinaesthetic learner!)

Each finger on both hands is numbered from 6 to 10, number 6 being the thumbs, moving outwards to number 10 being the little fingers.

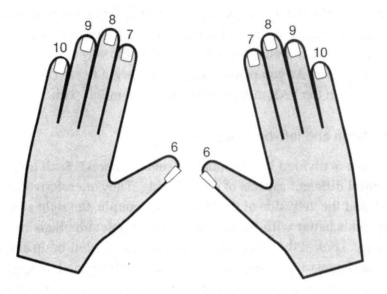

To do 7 × 8:

(a) Identify a 7 finger on one hand and an 8 finger on the other hand.
(b) Make a bridge by putting the 7 finger from one hand with the 8 finger from the other hand.
(c) From the bridge, **including those fingers making the bridge**, lower those fingers nearest to the body down on both hands, pinching them together as in the photo. Each one counts as a ten. In this case there are five fingers, so 5 × 10 = 50.
(d) The fingers left over and still sticking up, as in the photo, are: three on one hand and two on the other. **These have to be multiplied together** (3 × 2 = 6) and these are used as the units.
(e) So there are five tens (= 50) and 6 units. The answer is therefore 56.

Figure 1.6 *Learning times tables using the Romany Method*

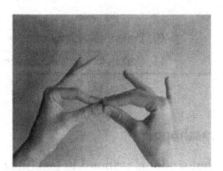

Figure 1.7 *Using the Romany Method*

Other learning style terms

Within this chapter, the VAK method of describing learning styles has been chosen as the most useful for you to observe and use. You may come across other methods used to describe the way students prefer to think and learn. As you read these you will begin to see that they overlap well with the VAK method you are now familiar with.

Right-brain and left-brain learners

The brain is divided into two halves (hemispheres). Each half is said to control different aspects of our thinking. They are referred to as the 'right' and the 'left' side of the brain. For example, the right side of the brain deals better with images, whereas the left side deals well with language. Look at the table below, used to describe left-brain and right-brain preferences. Are you strongly right- or left-brained, or a mixture? Can you see the similarities between this way of describing preferences and the VAK method?

Table 1.1 Left/right brain

Left (analytical)	Right (global)
1. Verbal	1. Visual
2. Responds to word meaning	2. Responds to tone of voice
3. Likes working in an ordered sequence	3. Random order of working
4. Information processed in a logical order	4. Information processed in a varied order
5. Responds to logic	5. Responds to emotion
6. Plans ahead	6. Impulsive
7. Recalls names of persons	7. Recalls people's faces
8. Speaks with few gestures	8. Gestures when speaking
9. Punctual	9. Less punctual
10. Prefers formal study design	10. Prefers sound/music background whilst studying
11. Prefers bright lights when studying.	11. Prefers frequent movement when studying

Inchworms and grasshoppers

The different way that students respond to tackling mathematics skills can be referred to as 'inchworms' and 'grasshoppers'(Chinn and Ashcroft 1998). Inchworms like to do things step by step in a logical sequence. They respond well to the rules of maths but find it difficult to picture or visualise the maths problem. Grasshoppers, on the other hand, can visualise instantly the whole problem. They are likely to be able to leap straight to the answer, intuitively. If you ask them how they got there they will have difficulty breaking it down into the sequenced steps. Strong inchworm students in grasshopper teaching classes are not usually successful. The link between the VAK method and left- and right-brained learners can be seen here also.

Remember that many students are flexible in their learning and thinking style; they can choose the most suitable one for the task in hand.

End-of-chapter checklist (tick when achieved)

☐ I understand the three different learning styles: V-A-K.

☐ I know my own preferred learning style.

☐ I have observed several students and identified their learning styles.

☐ I understand 'right-brain' and 'left-brain' preferences.

☐ I can identify 'grasshoppers' and 'inchworms' in maths lessons and can help them use their strengths.

☐ I have begun to allow kinaesthetic learners room to move and learn before writing.

☐ I recognise the importance of pictures, diagrams and colour to visual learners.

☐ I know to which pupils I need to explain the 'whole' task before concentrating on the detail.

☐ I know which students prefer the detail and sequence before seeing the whole task.

☐ I can show students the kinaesthetic method for learning the times tables.

☐ I have shown students how to use the times table visual method.

2 Developing independent learners

Chapter overview

When we are born we are totally dependent on others for survival. As we develop we gradually become more independent. To be successful in study involves becoming an independent learner. This requires a high level of 'intrapersonal skills' (knowing yourself). This chapter will look at what these skills are and your role in developing them in students. By the end of this chapter you will:

- understand your role in the classroom in developing these skills;
- support effective time management of class work, homework and extended coursework;
- have practical examples of how to encourage organisational skills development; and
- help students improve their work using the 'feedback sandwich'.

The better these skills are developed, the less a student will need you.

Towards an effective learner

Chapter 1 examined different learning styles and how these can improve success in school. However, there are several other factors involved in being successful. What else makes an effective learner, and how can knowing such skills help you to support your students? Howard Gardner (1983) – himself, at one time, a failed student who was forced to repeat a year of schooling – introduced the idea of multiple intelligences. He notes that there are several different types of intelligence. When we describe ourselves as 'clever' or 'average' or 'thick' we are usually measuring ourselves against only a small sample of these intelligence types, in particular the first two as described. Broadly, these intelligences are: analytical intelligence; pattern intelligence; musical intelligence; physical intelligence; practical intelligence; intrapersonal intelligence (knowing yourself) and inter-personal intelligence (getting on with others). You can see that different cultures may value the differing intelligences to a greater or lesser degree. Which intelligences are valued within our education system? Which intelligences do we as a society currently pay large sums of money to support? Which of these are strengths in yourself and the students you work with? How we value these intelligences in others, and praise them when we see them, affects our self-esteem and motivation.

Intrapersonal intelligence

Whatever your feelings with regard to the importance of each of these multiple intelligences and the importance you would place on having each one, there is no doubt that there is a need for intrapersonal intelligence in order to study successfully. Intrapersonal intelligence deals with a person's own ability to self-monitor, self-motivate and set targets. Some students find these skills develop naturally (if they have high levels of intrapersonal intelligence), but many students do not. They will need you to help set small targets for them and to celebrate when such targets have been reached. By doing this, both self-esteem and motivation will be raised and the student will become more successful. Within each of the areas discussed, this chapter encourages you to:

1. know where a student is in relation to each of the intrapersonal skills discussed;
2. set *one* small, achievable next-step target for *one* area;
3. create practical solutions to achieve it;
4. celebrate success when it is reached;
5. monitor the student in *maintaining* that success (this stage is often rushed past);
6. celebrate that maintenance;
7. return to 2 in a spiralling cycle of success.

Since we know that targets have a higher chance of success if they are written down, there is a template in the appendices for you to photo-copy and use (Appendix 2.1).

Managing time

Time management in the classroom

The awareness of time is called *temporal awareness*. Some students have a good feel for time; others do not. Students with specific learning difficulties, such as dyslexia or attention deficit disorder, whether

identified as having the difficulty or not, often have a very poorly developed sense of time. So when asked to get their books and equipment out in two minutes, or to complete what they are writing in the next ten minutes, they have difficulty. This does not mean they cannot tell the time, but that they find it difficult to judge time lapses. The Key Stage 3 Strategy, and the Literacy and Numeracy Strategy at Key Stage 2 have both helped, since students will have had plenty of experience of working in lessons divided into ten-minute starter sessions and 20 minutes working independently. These should be used as examples to support your students when given tasks to be completed in set times.

But what about the student who loses focus very quickly and starts chatting as soon as you are not there to focus them, or who finds it difficult to 'start off' and then ends up with piles of homework as a finishing-off task? Below is an example of how to use the spiralling target-setting described above.

The first target would be to know exactly how much the student is capable of writing when concentrating for ten minutes. (The amount for copying from the whiteboard or book would differ from the amount that could be written when creating their own written work, which needs additional thinking time.) This does not have to be completed as a separate exercise; you can use written examples from your observation of them across different subjects. Once you know how much they are capable of writing this can be used to set a target for self-management. You can then use time management strategies. When you are sure they are comfortable with the task you can draw a pencil line in their margin, which shows where they are up to, go away and come back later to see how much they have written. The amount of time they would be left to write independently should be short to begin with and should be increased. Each time target should be set, celebrated, monitored for maintenance across different subjects, celebrated and then increased. If when you return to the student they have not written enough (or anything) within their own capability, you need to discuss what they were doing instead, so that they know and recognise their own time-wasting behaviour. This may then become the target, for example: 'To write without chatting for . . . minutes'. What is important is that you gradually develop from always sitting beside the student to 'make them write' and move towards developing

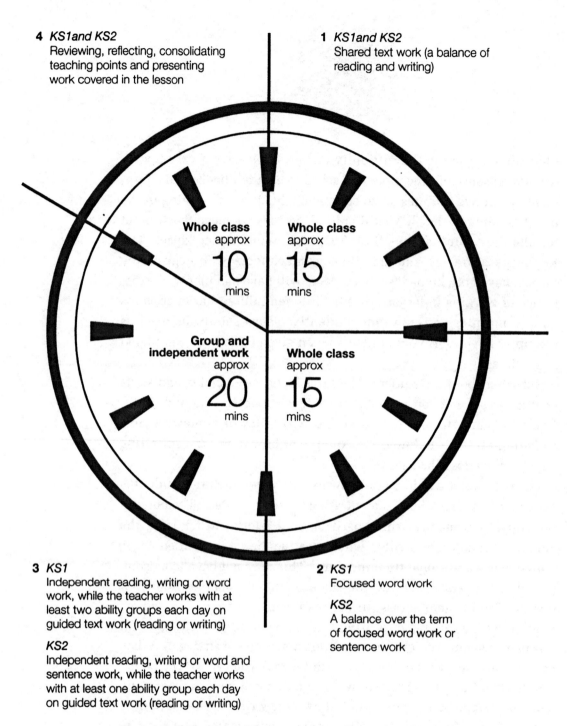

4 *KS1and KS2*
Reviewing, reflecting, consolidating teaching points and presenting work covered in the lesson

1 *KS1and KS2*
Shared text work (a balance of reading and writing)

Whole class
approx
10
mins

Whole class
approx
15
mins

Group and independent work
approx
20
mins

Whole class
approx
15
mins

3 *KS1*
Independent reading, writing or word work, while the teacher works with at least two ability groups each day on guided text work (reading or writing)

KS2
Independent reading, writing or word and sentence work, while the teacher works with at least one ability group each day on guided text work (reading or writing)

2 *KS1*
Focused word work

KS2
A balance over the term of focused word work or sentence work

Figure 2.1 *Structure of the Literacy Hour*

in them personal responsibility for 'making themselves write'. By the time a student can write for 15–20 minutes independently they should be well on the way to having achieved this intrapersonal skill. It may be necessary to use a timer, which could be the student's own watch, or rewards for targets achieved. Appropriate rewards will be discussed later in this chapter. A sample student target sheet is shown in Figure 2.2.

Some teachers use a rousing piece of music that lasts exactly two minutes: students must come into the room and get all of their equipment out on the desk before the music ends. They respond very well to this, especially as they become familiar with the piece. You may be able to suggest this to some of the teachers you work with.

Time management in the home

Time management skills take a long time to develop, and we learn from our own experiences about how long we need to finish different tasks. In addition, students with different learning styles (see Chapter 1) will wish to manage their time in different ways. This particularly affects how they manage their homework and extended coursework at GCSE. You will know of students who prefer to complete homework on the day it is set, and other students who prefer to leave homework till the night before it is due in. Neither style is right nor wrong if managed effectively, although they may not match *your* preferred style, so they may 'feel' wrong to you. So how can you help support time management skills with homework? First, knowing the amount a student can write independently, as discussed above, is crucial. This lets you know their speed of working, which is useful in helping support the student, parents, teachers and SENCOs set homework targets. Second, using the school homework organiser is crucial to homework time management. In my opinion it is essential to transfer the day on which the homework is due in, to *that* day in the homework organiser *as well as* the day on which it is completed. Many homework organisers have a 'due in' column. However, this does not help the 'just in time' student to visualise the amount of homework due in on one day if it is spread about several 'due in' columns. By transferring the homework to the 'due in' date, students can begin to see where lots of homework is piling up. This will enable them to prioritise their homework, rather than to start with the one they like or are good at. Otherwise, the 'just in time' strategy develops into 'not enough time'.

Prioritising homework

As students progress through Key Stage 3 to Key Stage 4 they will be given more homework with extended handing-in dates because it requires research, planning and redrafting skills. It is therefore essential that they begin to create their own priorities. Teach them to *prioritise* work in the time available. The most important work must be completed first. Ensure that students begin to recognise procrastination (putting things off) in themselves. We all procrastinate when faced with a task we find difficult. Being able to see that trait in yourself is an asset. (What do you do when you procrastinate? Do you hoover, tidy the house, check your e-mails?)

Target to be reached : To write without support for 10 minutes

Number of small steps planned : 5

Small step 1	What am I going to do to reach step one?	Date to reach target by	Target achieved	Target maintained for 2 weeks
Discover how much I write in 10 minutes when I concentrate	Choose a task where I know what to do. write without help for 10 minutes with the teaching assistant by me. Count the words	By the end of this week in one subject I am helped in.	(smiley face)	not needed.

Small step 2	What am I going to do to reach step one?	Date to reach target by	Target achieved	Target maintained for 2 weeks
To write for 3 minutes without help	Tell the T.A. I know what to do for the task, draw a pencil line and write on my own. Ask her to come back in 3 mins. Check I am still writing			

Small step 3	What am I going to do to reach step one?	Date to reach target by	Target achieved	Target maintained for 2 weeks
To write for 3 minutes without help in all lessons.	Take responsibility for knowing what I have to do. Draw my own pencil line and write for 3 minutes without checking			

Target to be reached : To write without support for 10 minutes Number of small steps planned : 5

Small step 4	What am I going to do to reach step one?	Date to reach target by	Target achieved	Target maintained for 2 weeks
To write on my own for 10 minutes in one lesson.	Choose the subject I work well in. Write for 10 minutes without help. Check with the T.A. that I have written enough.(target step 1)			
Small step	What am I going to do to reach step one?	Date to reach target by	Target achieved	Target maintained for 2 weeks
To write on my own in all lessons for 10 minutes.	Take personal responsibility for this final step.			
Small step	What am I going to do to reach step one?	Date to reach target by	Target achieved	Target maintained for 2 weeks
Target achieved. Choose next target.				

Figure 2.2 Sample student target sheet

Support them in planning extended pieces of work. Start with the date the work is due in and work *backwards* in the diary, putting in deadlines for the final write-up, handing in the draft, research period etc. By breaking the work up like this and working backwards they will be able to see the latest date at which they can *start* each small part of their work. Many students start GCSE coursework far too late, and only realise that they have not got enough time once they have started. It is then too late. If coursework makes up a high proportion of the marks, then the examiner expects to see that represented in *time* as well as *effort*.

Many of these priorities will be very personal and should be respected; for example the career route they may wish to follow, which means they give less time and effort to some homework areas and more to others; the study environment they have at home; and access to ICT for revision, research and writing up essays. Some homework may be best completed in school in their free time. Access to school computer suites is often prioritised for students nearing their exams. Your task is to support students in finding the best time to complete homework in the most suitable environment for their needs and to guide them if they are not planning ahead and prioritising well. A good example is a dance student who 'hated science' and said she wasn't 'too bothered' about her science coursework as she already had a place at dance school after GCSEs. As a student whose predicted grade was D/C, once she had it explained to her that should she ever wish to teach as part of her career in school she would need to have Science GCSE at Grade C or higher, this refocused her homework efforts with her science. This requires, flexibility, sensitivity, knowing the students you support and a discussion with subject teachers if you are unsure.

Footnote

Examine the timetable for the school you work in. Are there some instances when the student, and you, are required to be in two places at once, i.e. Maths 9.20-10.20, French 10.20–11.20. It is the case with some school timetables. Vast numbers of students are expected to transport themselves from one subject area to another with no time to do this. While teachers recognise this, and make some allowances for it, students need to know where these points are on their timetable and move swiftly to the next lesson.

Organisational skills

Do you recognise the story that goes with the picture of this student (Figure 2.3)? They arrive at the lesson late and flustered. They have brought the wrong exercise book (it is the correct colour, pink, but

Figure 2.3 *A disorganised student*

their History book, not their French book, which is also pink). They have lost their pen, although they had two when you were with them earlier in the day. The school bag is bulging with everything that the school curriculum may require, but not, it seems, the correct textbook. The teacher asks them to hand in their parent permission slip for the school trip next week, and they look dejected, because they were so excited about it but forget to give the slip to their parents. This is a familiar story for some students in secondary schools. If *you* find it frustrating, imagine how such students themselves find it. It lowers self-esteem, and the poor start to the lesson is demotivating.

The problems could be eased; you could carry a box of equipment and stationery to loan out. The teacher could always collect in exercise books and set homework on paper. Textbooks could not be allowed home. However, none of these develop intrapersonal skills, and so although they are quick fixes for the exasperated, which help lesson organisation, they do not develop the skills that students need. Developing organisational skills is an essential intrapersonal intelligence as you progress to adulthood: the pencil case will be replaced by a bank card; arriving late for work has more serious consequences than arriving late for a lesson; and losing a document you have worked on all week with colleagues more serious. So as a teaching assistant how can you help them develop?

The homework organiser

This is an essential tool in school. Students must take responsibility for it themselves. By using the staged target approach discussed above, they must be able to:

■ write in their own homework independently *exactly* as written by the teacher (just because they can remember at the time what to do with small, scribbled notes, it does not mean that they will later, particularly if they are a student who likes to leave homework until the day before the due-in date);

■ take responsibility for checking they understand the task or asking the teaching assistant or teacher for an explanation before the end of the lesson;

■ use a method to suit themselves, e.g. highlighter pens, to cross off in the diary when a homework assignment has been completed;

■ use a method to suit themselves to ensure they hand homework in on the correct day (as noted in time management);

■ find a suitable *study buddy* for additional 'emergency' support when stuck on homework. (A study buddy is not necessarily a close friend; it is a person in the same group that the student gets on with, with the same learning style, so they can explain things, by text, e-mail or a phone call, in the way that will be understood. They should have better organisational skills than the student they are helping.)

Remember that each of the bullet points is one target. Students with very poor organisational skills may need to improve all of them, but this takes time. Make your first choice the one that will improve self-esteem the most. This will motivate them to move on to the next target.

Organising equipment

Today's secondary school students are likely to end up with major back problems. They no longer use school desks to keep possessions in. Some schools have lockers, but the student with poor organisational skills will have lost the key to this. In addition, as they know they have poor organisational skills, they carry everything in their bag, not leaving anything at home in case it is needed. The result is a very heavy bag, which feeds the organisation problem as students lose equipment, notes and books in its depths. This is a priority intrapersonal skill that must be developed from Year 7. Bringing to school *only* what you *need* is essential. It may sound simple, but it shows *planning skills* and *time management skills* and, eventually, *self-confidence*. So how might the end target of packing their own bag with the correct equipment and books look like in the small-staged response for a student who refuses to move towards this skill? Below is a *suggested* order:

1. Select one day on the timetable where the lesson load is not complicated, i.e. no PE etc. Have that as the first target day for bringing only what is needed.

2. Decide if they are a morning or an evening person, including when they are less rushed, and decide to pack the bag in the evening or the next morning.

3. Stage 1: the student packs the bag with their parent or carer. Provide a small, laminated checklist if necessary. Celebrate success, with their parent or carer, when they tell you that they had everything they needed for that day or the next day. (If something was forgotten add to the checklist if necessary and repeat until achieved.)

4. Stage 2: the student packs their bag on their own for the same day. The bag is then checked for them, by their parent or carer. Celebrate success.

5. Maintain this and celebrate success.

6. The student packs their own bag, and does not have it checked.

7. Celebrate success, maintain and celebrate success.

8. Choose another, more complicated day. Repeat.

Experience shows that once students realise they can do this they will ride small disasters where they occasionally forget something, realising that this is normal. The following suggestions will also help those students with extremely poor organisational skills, who may live in disorganised family environments. For example, one characteristic of dyslexia is organisational skills difficulties. But dyslexia is hereditary, and so both parents may also find these skills a challenge too. Busy working parents with several children, all in different schools, may find it difficult to remember what each school's system is. You have no control over this, but you can provide suggestions, targets and appropriate rewards:

- Suggest the use of two pencil cases filled with cheap stationery. One is left at home for homework, the other permanently stays in the school bag. Lost equipment is replaced in the school pencil case each weekend and returned to the bag *immediately*.

- Use a box at home. Anything school-related found lying around the house is put into the box. This can help students who are hunting for an exercise book feel more at ease that it has probably been handed in for marking if it is not in their box.

- In school, whenever an exercise book is handed in, get them to write in their homework organiser on that day. Wipe the note through with a highlighter pen once the exercise book is given back to the student.

- Do not permanently lend out equipment; this de-skills a student. Lend it out occasionally but expect them to take responsibility for having equipment themselves.

All of these suggestions seem very simple. But a student who has their equipment, arrives to lessons on time, having completed their homework and handed it in on time, is becoming a student with good basic intrapersonal study skills.

Higher-level intrapersonal skills

Many students will display the basic intrapersonal skills that have been discussed so far. Higher-level intrapersonal skills will enable them to achieve their academic potential. These include motivation, persistence and the ability to act on constructive criticism and target-set from it.

Motivation

People are motivated in different ways. You have to know what motivates students. For some it is external rewards. This is because *rewarding* behaviour that you desire, rather than *punishing* and focusing on behaviour that you do not want, will always be more successful in improving intrapersonal skills. Behaviour does not just mean being good; behaviour means what you do, how you as an individual react in different situations.

External rewards

External rewards could be merit marks, achievement certificates, free time or even vouchers to use at popular stores. Some educators argue that all of these external rewards are poor at developing the correct motivational factors as part of a person's intrapersonal skills. However, for students who have only ever been punished, who have never achieved or have never known success, they are a useful first step. They are currently being used in some educational authorities to motivate students to improve their attendance, and hence their skills. You would also agree that as adults many of our motivations are external rewards. However, if external rewards are to be used as motivators they must maintain their value. Do not give stickers, merit marks or whatever is used within your school unless you know that it represents some sort of improvement or effort from that student in moving towards a target. Students do not need to be treated the same in order to be treated fairly. The end-product or behaviour will look different in each student as you give the reward, but the effort factor will be similar.

Internal motivation

Ultimately, internal motivation is one of the most useful intrapersonal skills to develop. It usually involves *delayed gratification*. This means putting off the reward until later while focusing on the task. That may mean staying in to study while your friends go out every night. It may mean switching off the television and making a start on your homework. Ultimately, in higher education, it often means going without money and getting into debt to realise your dreams. Delayed gratification is known to be one of the best indicators of future academic success even in children as young as three years. Would you have passed the chocolate experiment below?

Individual children were left alone in a room with one chocolate, but told that if they could wait until the adult came back into the room before eating the chocolate they could have two instead of one. The children fell into two groups: those who could wait for the two chocolates and those who could not, and who ate the chocolate as soon as the adult left the room. Both groups have been followed through until adulthood. The first group have been more successful academically when compared to children of similar intelligence.

Therefore, try to develop delayed gratification in the students you support. Try to point out to them internal rewards for what they are doing, as well as giving external rewards. Giving praise is more valuable to many students than a sticker or a merit mark.

Persistence

Thomas Edison invented the light bulb after 143 unsuccessful attempts. He was a very persistent man. We were all persistent as babies when learning to walk. We all will have fallen several times, but we got up and tried again and again until we could do it. So why is

this lost in some students? Students need to recognise if they give up easily. They may need help to be persistent. This often means pointing out small successes when all they see is failure. It includes not focusing on negative comments but on positive ones. It may involve encouraging them to have one more try than they would choose, and it most certainly means rewarding and praising persistence as an excellent behaviour rather than always rewarding end results.

Supporting students using the 'feedback sandwich'

You are in a privileged position. Students will often show you a piece of their work first before handing it to a teacher. They commonly ask you, 'Is this okay?' So how can you answer honestly, so that you tell them what is good about their work and also help them by suggesting ways it could be improved, thus moving them forward without damaging their self-esteem? The answer is the 'feedback sandwich'.

What is a 'feedback sandwich?'

When a student has worked very hard on a piece of work it is really difficult for them to accept some constructive comments that would improve it. In addition, when you have seen how hard they have worked it is difficult to offer this support. But instant verbal feedback is really useful for students. You need to talk to them about their work carefully. Self-esteem is easily damaged and the wrong comment at the wrong time can be demotivating. The feedback sandwich allows you to offer useful instant oral support. The constructive criticism, which will move the student on, is *sandwiched* between two positive comments and praise for the work. This means that the first and last thing that the student hears you talk about in relation to their work is positive. This keeps self-esteem intact and they are more likely to accept and act on the suggestions you offer in the middle of the sandwich to improve it.

It may sound like this:

'You have looked really carefully at the essay title and answered it exactly the way you need to. Your introduction is very interesting. It makes me want to read on.'

'You could improve the conclusion by making it a separate paragraph that sums up what you have decided to agree with. At the moment I cannot see your final decision clearly.'

'Wow, does that really happen when they fox hunt? I didn't know that. You have taught me something new today. You have really learnt a lot during this essay. You must have read lots about it before you started writing.'

Figure 2.4 *The 'feedback sandwich'*

Written feedback

Most written comments to students will contain comments of praise and constructive criticism. You may need to reorder them for the student into the shape of the feedback sandwich if they feel unhappy or dejected when they receive written feedback.

Marks and grades in homework, assessments and tests have two purposes. The first purpose is to let the teacher and the student know what level that they are performing at. The second purpose is far more important: it allows the teacher and the student to know, within that level, what they are good at and which areas to focus on next in order to improve. For example, it is not much use knowing you have achieved level 5 in the Key Stage 3 Maths SAT unless you also know where your strengths and weaknesses are within the areas of shape and space, numeracy, algebra and data handling. Therefore comments and feedback on homework, coursework, essays and exams are important. If all of the comments are praise, then the student knows what they did correctly for the grade, but they do not know the next step needed to move one grade higher. If comments are all negative, then the student knows what they did wrong that prevented a higher grade, but they do not know which parts of their work were good and so will not know which aspects of their learning and skills to change and which ones to keep the same. Teachers are skilled in giving feedback and it usually comes in the form of the 'feedback sandwich'. There will be some praise, showing what was good and what has been achieved, followed by some constructive criticism showing what the focus needs to be, followed by a final comment of praise. Higher-order intrapersonal skills involve studying the feedback carefully. Many of them just look at the grade and put the work away. Both praise and constructive criticism need to be analysed. The student then needs to accept the support and, together with the teacher and the teaching assistant, plan the target for the next step. In many instances this target will be transferable to several areas of the curriculum. Look at the following written feedback sandwiches for the same student. How would you explain to this student what they were good at and what their next step needs to be?

> You have clearly learned a lot about volcanoes. You have described the effects they have on people well. The question also asked you to look at the benefits of living near a volcano in detail. Your case study information was detailed enough which suggested you revised well.

> I wonder why you have written this as a letter? The question asked you to explain in detail the benefits of a chosen career. Your essay flows well and you have some good ideas but you have lost marks by lack of detail and using the style of a letter.

In both cases the student clearly has the ability to write well. In both instances they have demonstrated that they have the correct subject knowledge. But in both comments you can see that they have misread or misinterpreted the question and that their answers lack detail.

This student probably revised well. He/she is probably good at retaining information. Currently he/she needs to focus on developing answers in more detail (see Chapter 4). He/she also needs to learn how to read questions in exams (see Chapter 6). If this was a Year 10 student, what would you focus on first as a target and why? What else might you also want to know before deciding?

This chapter has looked at some of the social and psychological factors that affect studying. As a teaching assistant many of these are outside your control, but understanding their effect on study and how you can intervene to provide effective support is important. Sometimes good support means taking a step back and allowing a student to accept responsibility for himself and his learning.

End-of-chapter checklist (tick when achieved)

☐ I understand that targets need small steps planning.

☐ I have planned and supported a student in achieving a target using small steps.

☐ I am aware of the difference between intrapersonal and interpersonal skills.

☐ I am aware that different students are motivated by either external or internal rewards.

☐ I understand the school's reward system.

☐ I know which students require external rewards and use them fairly.

☐ I understand delayed gratification.

☐ I have used the 'feedback sandwich' when a student asks me for advice about their work.

☐ I have supported a student in reviewing a teacher's written feedback using the feedback sandwich.

# Higher-order reading skills

Chapter overview

> The true purpose of reading is not in decoding the words but in understanding the content, so that reading for pleasure or for information becomes the predominant activity. By the end of this chapter you will be able to:
>
> - understand the hierarchy of comprehension skills and apply this to how you ask students questions to improve their understanding of texts;
> - use active techniques to assist students in extracting the key ideas from texts; and
> - develop note-taking skills.

Introduction

Perhaps the most fundamental recent shift in society today is that it is essential to be literate. The twenty-first century is the information age and alongside this has come an explosion in the amount and variety of reading material that we are all bombarded with on a daily basis. This presents us with challenges. Is the information I have received true? Does it contain technical language that I am not familiar with? Is it factual, and if so, does it contain all of the facts I need? Does the text contain opinions as well as facts. Are these opinions biased? Is this text trying to persuade me? All of these are examples of what is meant by higher-order reading skills.

Education reflects these changes and is aimed at encouraging students to use such skills. Therefore the Key Stage 3 and Key Stage 4 curriculum offers several opportunities for students to develop their skills. Higher-order reading skills promote good thinking skills, but not all students develop them automatically. In some instances students are so busy decoding the text that they have little capacity to think about the content of the material they are reading. This chapter will help you to develop these skills in students you work with.

Asking students the right questions (quality not quantity)

A hierarchy of reading comprehension

The term 'hierarchy' simply means the way that people or things are ranked or positioned in order of importance. In History, at Key Stage 3, students learn about the hierarchy of the feudal system as shown below. Very often they are introduced to the idea of hierarchies by working out the hierarchy of people in their own school.

KING

↓

BISHOPS

↓

BARONS

↓

LORDS

↓

PEASANTS

Figure 3.1 *The feudal system*

When we talk about a hierarchy of comprehension skills we are concerned with the level of thinking required in order to understand and/or answer questions related to reading material. By recognising that the quality of questioning can improve a student's ability to understand the text, you can learn to ask students questions of gradually increasing difficulty. This is known as 'reading yourself into the text' or 'reading the writer out of the text'. In addition, it helps students to recognise that questions asked of them can be of varying degrees of difficulty. Most important of all, it should help to surmount the age-old problem of students saying 'I can't answer the question because it doesn't say . . .'.

Below is a hierarchy for comprehension questions. This hierarchy starts with the lowest and easiest level and ends with the highest level. It is important to remember that these hierarchies are only *models*; they have been put together by educationalists so that we can have a framework around which we can discuss students' skills. You may come across other models that differ slightly from this.

Activity 1

Before looking at the hierarchy below, read this short passage from *Skellig*, by David Almond, a popular Year 7 novel:

I found him in the garage on a Sunday afternoon. It was the day after we moved into Falconer Road. The winter was ending. Mum had said we'd be moving just in time for spring. Nobody else was there. Just me. The others were inside the house with Doctor Death, worrying about the baby.

He was lying there in the darkness behind the chests, in dust and dirt. It was as if he'd been there forever. He was filthy and pale and dried out and I thought he was dead. I couldn't have been more wrong. I'd soon begin to see the truth about him, that there'd never been another creature like him in the world. (Almond 1998)

Literal comprehension

Answers to literal comprehension questions can be lifted straight from the text. The text does not need to be rearranged, although the question may be made slightly more difficult by changing the vocabulary. Literal questions for the text above may be: What day did this happen? What time of year is it? What is the name of the road?

Literal questions are quite acceptable, they help students to visualise the text (see Chapter 1 on teaching and learning styles). They are often used at the beginning of comprehension exercises or exam questions to settle a student and, as noted above, help to read them into the text. However, they do have weaknesses; because students can lift the answer from the text they are not a very good way of monitoring a student's understanding. Students can become very skilled at the mechanics of literal comprehension without ever really understanding the text.

Comprehension reorganisation

Such questions are still relatively simple. However, they may require the student to collect information from several places in the passage and put it together. They are therefore useful in encouraging a student to read the whole text. The important point is that all of the information is still within the text. A comprehension reorganisation question from the short extract above may be:

Which characters have been introduced to the reader in the opening passage of this book?

Inferential comprehension

This consists of looking beyond the reading. It is often referred to as 'reading between the lines'. Students must use the information from the passage, but in addition they must add to that their own experiences in order to respond to the question. Most students at the beginning of Key Stage 3 find the transition from literal and comprehension organisation questions to inferential questions very difficult, and need to be encouraged to take this step. Try to ask lots of inferential questions of students so that they are less fearful of them. They can be referred to as 'Dig Deep' questions (the student needs to think harder). Help students to recognise them in textbooks, exam questions and in teacher questioning activities. Inferential comprehension questions for the passage above may be:

Do you think Doctor Death is the doctor's real name?

How ill is the baby? Why do you think this?

Evaluation

Here, quite high levels of thinking are required. The student must make their own judgements about the text and compare criteria within the passage to external criteria. They must begin to be aware of bias, purpose and the audience the text was written for (see Chapter 4 on essay-writing skills). Typical evaluation questions include asking students:

Could this really have happened?

Was this right or wrong?

What do you think they should have done?

(And personal responses to the writing.)

An evaluation question for the example above may be:

In what way does the opening of this story encourage you to read on? What is interesting about this story opening?

Notice the first question is phrased in such a way that the student cannot give you a one-word response, known as an open question. If the question had been 'Does the opening of the story encourage you to read on?' the student would have been able to give you a yes/no answer which would not enable you to see if there was some evaluative thinking behind their answer. Try to avoid questions that allow a yes/no response which are known as closed questions.

Appreciation

This is the highest level of thinking. By Key Stage 4 all students will be expected to demonstrate these skills in response to their reading, particularly in the Humanities subjects and in English. (Of course, many students at Key Stage 3 begin to demonstrate these skills.) Appreciation involves being able to assimilate what the writer had in mind when writing the particular text. It requires being aware of the author's intentions and being aware of the type (genre) of writing. This enables you as the reader to be aware of the author's bias, whether the facts presented to you represent a selection of facts or a balanced view and whether the author is trying to persuade you of their point of view. Every time we read a newspaper article we are (or should be) interacting with the text at the appreciation level. We have to be able to evaluate the information and decide on its use and 'truthfulness'. There is insufficient text in our example to be able to ask a useful appreciation question.

Activity 2

Read the two articles below. One is from a Key Stage 3 History textbook where the level of reading difficulty has been controlled. The other is from the *Oxford Interactive Encyclopaedia*, where the reading level is harder. However, it is typical of the sort of article a student may bring to a lesson in response to a research or 'find out about' homework.

Using the hierarchy above, once you have read the articles, design a series of questions that you could use to help a student gain understanding from both texts. (A sample set of hierarchy questions are shown overleaf for further practice if needed. You will have several more suggestions.)

In Appendix 3.1 at the end of this book you will find a list of suitable questions for each level of the hierarchy. You may find it useful to photocopy this for use across the curriculum.

Article 1: the murder of Thomas Becket

On 29 December 1170, the Archbishop of Canterbury, Thomas Becket, was murdered in Canterbury Cathedral. The four knights who carried out the murder claimed that they were acting on orders from the king. How could such a terrible thing have happened?

Becket had been appointed Archbishop by Henry II in 1162. He and Henry had been friends for many years and the king expected that the new Archbishop would support him in everything he did. But Becket had strong views on the importance of the Church.

Medieval priests did not always behave as we would expect priests today to behave. Some of them committed crimes and had to be punished. But these priests could ask to be tried by the Church's own courts and often got light sentences. Henry did not like this, and passed new laws saying priests should be tried in the king's courts like everyone else. Becket said Henry was interfering with the rights of the Church. He and Henry quarrelled so strongly that, in 1165, Becket left England.

Becket returned in 1170 and he and Henry tried to work together. But Becket was cross about what had happened. He immediately excommunicated (expelled from the church) all those bishops who had been helping Henry while he was abroad. The King could hardly believe it. In his anger he is said to have shouted: 'Will no-one rid me of this turbulent priest?' Four knights decided that Henry wanted Becket dead, and they murdered him. Henry later claimed that he had not meant that at all.

Soon people began to believe that miracles were happening at the spot where Becket died. The Pope announced Becket would be called a saint and people came from far and wide to pray at the tomb of St Thomas, 'God's holy martyr'.

Article 2

Becket, Thomas à, St (1118–70), Archbishop of Canterbury (1162–70). Born in London, and educated in Paris and Bologna, Becket became archdeacon of Canterbury (1154) shortly before Henry II made him Chancellor of England (1155), and he served the King as statesman and diplomat. However, when Becket became Archbishop (1162) he became a determined defender of the rights of the Church. He came into conflict with the King in the councils of Westminster, Clarendon and Northampton (1163–4), particularly over Henry's claim to try in the lay courts clergy who had already been convicted in the ecclesiastical courts. Refusing to endorse the Constitutions of Clarendon (1164), Becket went into exile in France. On his return (1170), apparently reconciled to Henry, Becket suspended those Bishops who had accepted these Constitutions. Henry's rage over this action was misinterpreted by four knights who assumed he would approve their murder of Becket. Acclaimed a martyr, and canonised (1173), his shrine became a centre of Christian pilgrimage.
(*Oxford Interactive Encyclopaedia* 1997)

Literal questions

Who was Thomas Becket?

Where was Thomas Becket murdered?

Who murdered Thomas Becket?

When did Becket return from exile?

What does 'excommunicated' mean? (see previous comments about the disadvantages of literal comprehension questions; it is easy to answer this and yet not know what 'expelled' means either!)

Comprehension reorganisation

Make a time-line of important events in Thomas Becket's life until his death.

Name two places where priests could be tried if they did something wrong.

Inferential comprehension

Why did the knights decide to murder Thomas Becket?

Why do you think Thomas decided to suspend the bishops who had followed Henry's court laws?

Why do you think Thomas returned from France in 1170?

Evaluation

Do you think King Henry II wanted Becket killed? Give reasons for your answer.

In medieval society what would people's reactions to a murder within a cathedral be?

Who was most to blame for Becket's death: Henry II, Thomas Becket or the four knights?

Analysis

The article from the encyclopaedia states that the knights 'misinterpreted' Henry's rage. Why do you think the writer chose this word?

The writer in the first article writes, 'Soon people began to believe that miracles were happening at the spot where Becket died.'

How does the use of the word 'believe' show you that this is written for an information text?

Getting to grips with reading and note-taking

Active techniques to assist students in extracting the key ideas from texts

When you ask students if they have read anything out of school that day they often answer 'no', and that they don't like reading. The fact is that they will have undertaken lots of reading. If you ask them to make a list it may include:

- reading a text message they have received;
- using 'teletext' to chose the evening's television viewing;
- reading the sports page of the newspaper;
- checking their homework diary and timetable;
- reading a magazine;
- checking a bus timetable.

The list is endless. Reading is a varied skill. Within this chapter we are going to divide reading skills into four groups. We will look at the first three reading skills in detail. Close reading will be discussed in Chapter 6, linked to examination techniques. Although some of the terminology may be new to you, students will have looked at these reading skills as part of their Key Stage 2 National Literacy Strategy. It may be useful to remind them that they have used these skills before:

1. scanning
2. skimming
3. reading for information
4. close reading.

1. Scanning skills

When scanning, we are looking over a text very quickly to try to locate a key piece of information. This could be a key number, a key word or a phrase. Text layouts often help students to scan by putting key words in **bold**, *italics or* <u>underlining</u>. They may also use coloured type. In today's computer game playing, TV channel hopping and visual world, most students now have well-developed scanning skills. Help them to recognise this as one of their key learning strengths and *transfer* these skills for use in their reading at school.

2. Skimming (work smarter, not harder)

The Key Stage 2 National Literacy Strategy states that skimming is 'to read to get an initial overview of the subject matter and main ideas of the passage'. How then do you do this, and why bother? It is back to our WIIFM (the key question of 'What's in it for me?').

You need to be able to persuade students that by skimming they will *save* time. Skimming is a 'work smarter, not harder' technique.

■ *Read the title*. This may seem obvious, but the next time you are sitting with students and ask them to read the passage aloud to you, observe where they start. It is very rarely with the title. So why bother to read the title as part of skimming? What if the title was 'Mars'? Did you start to think of planets and the solar system or did you start to think of chocolate? Reading the title starts to let your brain *collect together* all of the other information it may *already know* about the subject (and to check you are thinking about the correct subject where there are ambiguities). This is vital for reading and understanding. New knowledge needs to find the correct 'hook' on which to hang. Each student will already know something, and by asking them to read the title and *talk about* what they already know from reading just that, they will understand the text more. Hence they will be able to attach new information and learning to familiar places and be able to get it back out (retrieve it) more easily when needed. (Retrieval of information is discussed in Chapter 5 in 'Managing memory').

■ *Read the subheadings* (if there are any). Not only does this have the same effect as reading the title, it also helps students to know how many parts there are to the information they have to read. For example, if the title is 'Mars' and there are three subtitles, the student knows instantly that there are three main facts that they will need to consider about the topic of Mars.

■ *Count the paragraphs within the text.* If there are six paragraphs within the text then there are six pieces of information. Students often know, when they write, that each paragraph must be linked to the same topic. They often fail to *transfer* this knowledge to their reading.

■ *Highlight the first sentence in each paragraph.* All good paragraphs start with a key sentence. This is sometimes known as a 'power sentence'. (Some first sentences may be quite long and so can be highlighted up to the first comma.) Using a highlighter pen highlight each key sentence. (It is not always possible to highlight the text (if it is in a school textbook you would not be very popular). However, an acetate sheet can be clipped over any textbook using paper clips, and *that* can be highlighted. Highlighting is an active strategy and involves the student. On some occasions the first sentence in a paragraph does not appear to be the key sentence. If this is the case, you need to look at the paragraph *above* and read its *last* sentence. Often writers use the last sentence of a paragraph to prepare the reader for a topic in the next paragraph.

■ *Highlight the key word within the key sentence.* This is best completed with a different coloured highlighter pen. Look at the key sentence again and select one or two words from that sentence that represent the key idea. Some students find it difficult to select one or two words and so highlight too much. They need help and the confidence to improve this skill.

■ *Now read out loud the title*, saying one thing you already know about the subject, saying how many subheadings there are and reading aloud the key sentence from each paragraph and stating what you think the key word is. All of this should be completed reasonably quickly, but it is important to count, highlight and read aloud. These allow for *metacognition* (an educational word meaning 'thinking about thinking').

Using the short article 'Why do people live near volcanoes?' practise your skimming skills.

Why do people live close to volcanoes?

Volcanoes have a wide range of effects on humans. These can be problematic or beneficial. It is usually the destructive nature of volcanoes that is more widely documented. However, many people rely on volcanoes for their everyday survival. Today, many millions of people live close to volcanoes for this very reason.

People live close to volcanoes because Geothermal energy can be harnessed by using the steam from underground which has been heated by the Earth's magma. This steam is used to drive turbines in geothermal power stations to produce electricity for domestic and industrial use. Countries such as Iceland and New Zealand use this method of generating electricity.

Volcanoes attract millions of visitors around the world every year. Apart from the volcano itself, hot springs and geysers can also bring in the tourists. This creates many jobs for people in the tourism industry, including work in hotels, restaurants and gift shops. Often locals are also employed as tour guides.

Lava from deep within the earth contains minerals, which can be mined once the lava has cooled. These include gold, silver, diamonds, copper and zinc, depending on their mineral composition. Often mining towns develop around volcanoes.

Volcanic areas often contain some of the most mineral-rich soil in the world. This is ideal for farming. Lava and material from pyroclastic flows are weathered to form nutrient rich soil, which can be cultivated to produce healthy crops and rich harvests. (www.geography.learnontheinternet.co.uk/topics/volcanoes)

Did you:

- read the title and state one fact you already knew;
- count five paragraphs and therefore appreciate that there were five things you needed to understand;
- highlight the key sentence in each paragraph;
- reduce each key sentence to a key word using a different pen?

The key fact about the title could be: lots of people do, so there must be some good reason. Key words in each paragraph could be:

1. effects on humans are good and bad, so what's good?

2. geothermal energy

3. visitors (this may have been changed by some geographers to the key word 'tourism')

4. lava – minerals

5. rich soil.

3. Reading for information

Note-taking

Students are usually asked to either answer questions on texts they have read or to make notes from them in preparation for their own writing. You have already noted above the different types of questioning. The level of questions can now be pointed out to students, and they should practise recognising when a difficult level of question has been asked.

Preventing students from just copying out the first paragraph

You will be familiar with students who, when asked to take notes, copy out the first paragraph or huge chunks of the text without using their own language and interacting with the text at all. This is totally passive; you can almost see it coming in through their eyes and out through their arm and hand without going through the brain. The only golden rule is that *note-taking requires active strategies*. There is no right or wrong way to make notes; there are different methods that suit different students and those methods are useful with different texts. (See Chapter 1 on teaching and learning styles.)

To support students you may need to develop note-taking techniques that you do not like yourself as they do not suit your own learning style. The important point is to take time, trial various techniques with different students and help them to recognise which ones best suit them. All note-taking techniques will involve skimming skills initially. Below are some useful techniques and examples of students' work.

Using the six Ws

The six Ws are: Where, What, When, Who, Why and How. ('How' is a little misleading as the w is at the end, but students often confuse the spelling of 'who' and 'how' so it is an additional tool to help sort this out.) Students use the key W words to reduce the information. By using 'why' and 'how' words in the note-taking you will encourage students to grapple with the harder concepts in the text. To begin with you may wish to use a writing frame to support students in extracting information in this way. The writing frame (Appendix 4.2) may be photocopied. It can also be enlarged to A3 and laminated.

Having skimmed their text, students can now place small parts of the information in the correct category. (The circles on the six Ws frame allow students to rank the information in order of importance by numbering them, once they have made short notes.)

Below is an example of the frame used to take notes from the articles above on the murder of Thomas Becket.

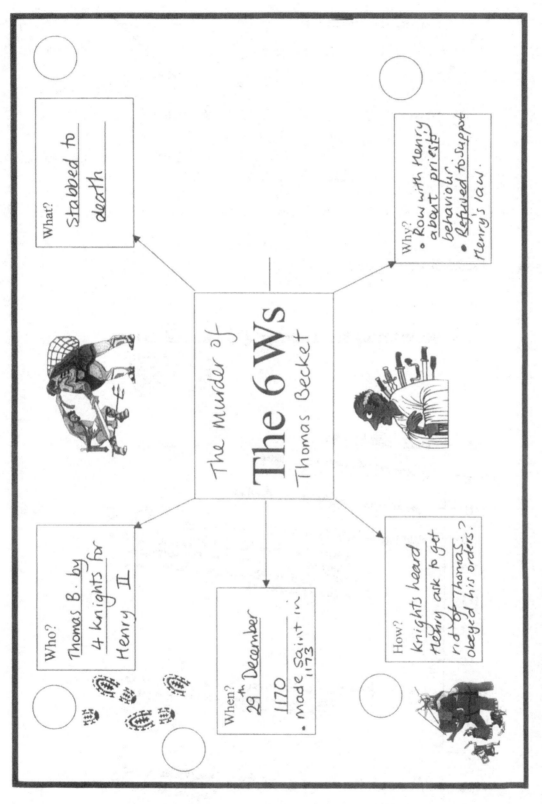

Figure 3.2 *Writing frame for Thomas à Becket*

When did the joust entertain?

Planning using the 6ws

What are tapestries?

when?

what?

where?

Who were the rulers?

who?

Where were the garderobes?

why?

how?

How were arguments solved?

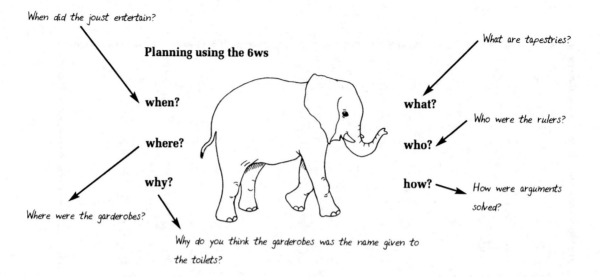

Why do you think the garderobes was the name given to the toilets?

Figure 3.3 A sticker to help using the 6 Ws

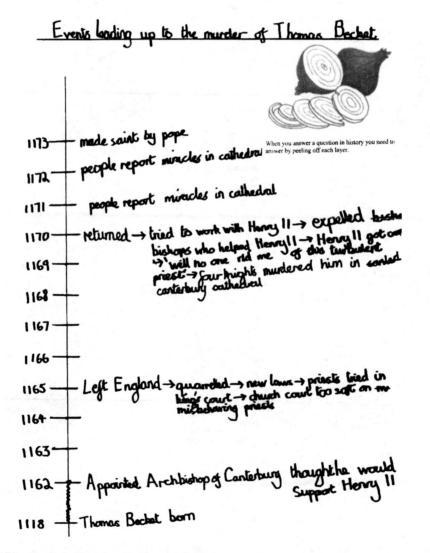

Events leading up to the murder of Thomas Becket.

When you answer a question in history you need to answer by peeling off each layer.

1173 — made saint by pope

1172 — people report miracles in cathedral

1171 — people report miracles in cathedral

1170 — returned → tried to work with Henry II → expelled bishops who helped Henry II → Henry II got cross → 'will no one rid me of this turbulent priest' → four knights murdered him in canterbury cathedral

1169 —

1168 —

1167 —

1166 —

1165 — Left England → quarrelled → new laws → priests tried in king's court → church court too soft on misbehaving priests

1164 —

1163 —

1162 — Appointed Archbishop of Canterbury thought he would support Henry II

1118 — Thomas Becket born

Figure 3.4 Time-line for Thomas Becket

Figure 3.5 *Picture method for Thomas Becket*

Once familiar with the six Ws, students should be able to use them without the frame. Initially stickers may be used as a transition phase, in exercise books, as is shown in Figure 3.3.

The aim is to enable students to become independent learners who can make notes without your help. Do not be shy of telling them to try out skills on their own once you are sure they have been taught them. Being an effective teaching assistant involves knowing when to let go as well as when to hold on.

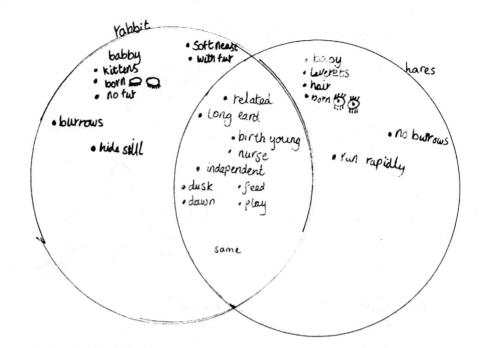

Figure 3.6 *Venn diagram*

Time-lines

Students who are left-brained learners (see Chapter 1 on teaching and learning styles) may prefer to use linear notes (those made in a logical line). Below is an example of a time-line of notes made by a student using the same text as above.

Drawing pictures

Many students are visual learners; they find it difficult to remember words they have read. However, once converted to visual images, they can understand the text and use their notes much more effectively. Students using exercise books can fold the page length-ways in half. Small keyword notes are placed in the left-hand column, taken from their skimming. The right-hand column is used to supplement the words with drawings and symbols. It is important to use a few key words, since they will be vital for use in their writing or for exams. They are also likely to be the new vocabulary, or dates within a text that need to be learned for meaning and spelling. Below is an example of the picture method for the Thomas Becket articles. (Humour helps understanding and memory.)

Venn diagrams

These are useful when students need to take notes on the *similarities* and *differences* in texts (for example, the similarities and differences between two poems in English, two religions in RS, two species of animals in Science, two sports in PE etc.).

First, the student needs three different-coloured highlighter pens. Two of the colours are used to highlight the key differences separately. The third colour is used to highlight similarities. Once highlighted, the notes are transferred to a large Venn diagram (preferably using the same colours with pencils or felt pens). Students who are visual learners find this is a useful note-taking technique. The example below shows a student's Venn diagram made from an article discussing the similarities and differences between hares and rabbits.

Mind mapping

Students who are right-brained tend to prefer notes that are non-linear. Mind mapping is a useful way of reducing text to key words and adding pictures, colour and symbols. How to mind map is discussed again in Chapter 5. It is now a familiar tool in most schools; many students will have been taught the principle of mind mapping during Key Stage 2.

The advantages of mind mapping are:

- it can be fun;
- it uses the whole brain, so it suits left- and right-brained individuals;
- words or pictures can be used;
- it is very active learning;
- it builds upon skimming skills – three subheadings guide you to draw three main branches. Three paragraphs within one subheading means three mini-branches to draw within that branch;
- it forces the reader to confront difficult sections of the text in order to mind map it. Some methods allow you to just skip harder sections.

The disadvantages are that:

- it is time-consuming;
- pre-drawn mind maps are often given to students. This defeats their object. The note taking has become passive again;
- mind mapping is sometimes forced on students who do not find it useful;
- it needs A3 paper, which can present students with organisational difficulties in books and folders;
- it is confused with spidergrams. Spidergrams are less organised and look more like the six Ws sticker response above. Mind maps *organise* the information into more and less important points.

Below are two examples of students' mind maps. One is hand drawn; the other uses ICT technology discussed in Chapter 7.

Cloze procedures

This is a method of note-taking that you may see used in school, in textbooks, on worksheets and in exam questions. In cloze procedures key words are removed from the text and gaps are left in their place. Students are asked to replace the gaps with suitable words. On some

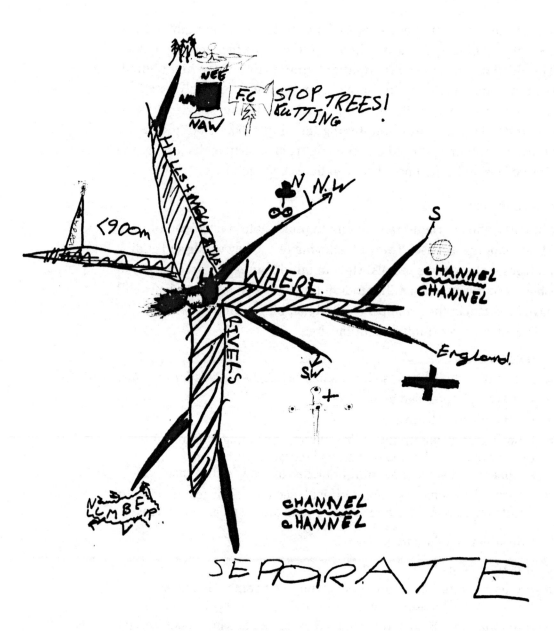

Figure 3.7 *A hand-drawn mind map*

occasions the words that need to be used are placed at the bottom of the text. On other occasions students are expected to use their own words.

The advantages are:

- they are useful for reluctant writers who find it difficult to write large amounts of text;
- they ensure that notes in students' books are accurate, providing the key words are checked;
- they ensure students focus on the key words for spelling and meaning.

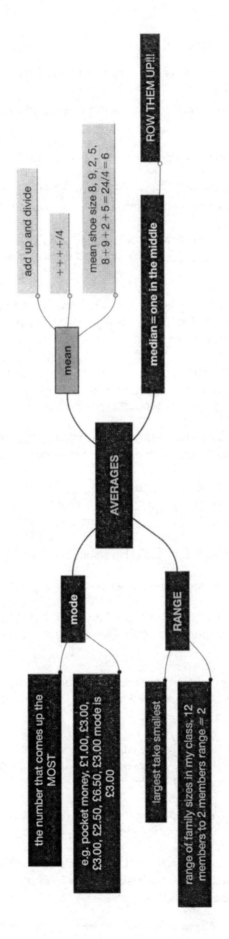

Figure 3.8 A computer-drawn mind map

The disadvantages are that:

- they are a reasonably passive technique which does not promote understanding;
- they de-skill students from being independent note-takers.

An example of a cloze procedure is shown below.

LAY OFF BECKS! HE NEEDS THE FANS' SUPPORT, NOT ABUSE.
Now is the time for every football fan to ___ behind David Beckham.

That applies to all those watching _____ 2000 from their armchairs just as it does every _____ in Holland and Belgium now, or those planning to _____.

The match against Germany in Charleroi on Saturday is ____biggest England has faced since the heart-break of World Cup _____ against Argentina at France 98.

But for England to _____ any chance of turning around the disappoint-ment of defeat by _____ in the opening match of Euro 2000, every player _____ every supporter behind them.

Beckham, who suffered humiliation when _____was sent off against Argentina, is once again in the _____ for all the wrong reasons.

The picture of the Manchester United _____ boy raising his middle finger in the direction of England _____ after the 3-2 defeat by Portugal on Monday has been _____ around the world.

LAY OFF BECKS! HE NEEDS THE FANS' SUPPORT, NOT ABUSE.

Now is the time for every football fan to get behind David Beckham.

That applies to all those watching Euro 2000 from their armchairs just as it does every supporter in Holland and Belgium now, or those planning to travel.

The match against Germany in Charleroi on Saturday is the biggest England has faced since the heart-break of World Cup elimination against Argentina at France 98.

But for England to stand any chance of turning around the disappointment of defeat by Portugal in the opening match of Euro 2000, every player needs every supporter behind them.

Beckham, who suffered humiliation when he was sent off against Argentina, is once again in the news for all the wrong reasons.

The picture of the Manchester United golden boy raising his middle finger in the direction of England fans after the 3–2 defeat by Portugal on Monday has been flashed around the world.

End-of-chapter checklist (tick when achieved)

☐ I can recognise the different levels of questions in textbooks and during class discussions.

☐ I can use the hierarchy of questions to ask my own students questions to ensure they understand their text.

☐ The students I work with can now ask questions of differing levels when talking about a text.

☐ I know the difference between open and closed questions.

☐ I have started to use more open questions when working with students.

☐ I know the difference between scanning and skimming.

☐ My students always read the title when looking at new texts.

☐ I am using active techniques to develop skimming skills.

☐ I am familiar with a range of note-taking skills.

☐ My own preferred note-taking skill is.....................

☐ I have begun to suggest particular note-taking skills to match individuals' learning styles.

 **Extended writing skills**

Chapter overview

Writing skills demand so much of students, rather like the ability of a conductor to manage several things at once while conducting an orchestra. During Key Stages 3 and 4 students must develop extended writing skills, and this, too, involves managing several tasks at once. They must focus at the word level on their choice of vocabulary and spelling and ensure that what they have written is legible. Their sentences must be constructed well and put together in paragraphs so that the writing flows easily. Finally, the writing as a whole must engage with the audience in an appropriate style. Many students demonstrate that they have learned and understood the subject matter orally but cannot express their thoughts on paper. Their written work shows disorganised thinking, the content lacks depth and they do not have the ability to sequence essays logically. By the end of this chapter you will be able to support students with their writing at the word, sentence and text level by:

- identifying the key aims of written assignments;

- brainstorming ideas for essays, using techniques to match students' preferred learning styles;

- organising ideas into a plan using key words and 'power sentences';

- learning about different writing frames, their advantages and disadvantages;

- helping students to write in detail by structuring paragraphs using the mnemonic 'siege'; and

- developing active techniques for draft checking work by separating the process into two distinct areas: authorial and secretarial skills.

Identifying the key aims of written assignments

In Chapter 3 we discussed that students read as part of their everyday life far more than perhaps they realise. This is also the case with writing, for example sending text messages, talking in internet 'chat rooms', compiling shopping lists and leaving written reminders of telephone messages for other family members. These are all informal types of written communication. However, since writing is still the most widely used method of assessing a student's learning in school, they must be able to write formally, across different subject areas. So how can you support a student in developing a range of writing styles? One way is to analyse carefully before any writing can begin, and to do this it is essential that all written tasks start with a 'PAS' (**P**urpose, **A**udience, **S**tructure).

Purpose

All writing has a purpose – the reason for the writing. This purpose does not mean 'Because that is what the teacher has asked me to do'. Students need to look beyond this. For example, is the purpose of the writing to *explain* how the water cycle works, or to give *instructions*, as with a recipe? Is it to *persuade*, as in a Religious Education essay that argues the case for or against abortion, or a poster that persuades students to stop smoking as part of their Citizenship course? It is most important that you think about the purpose of any written task that students have been given, as this will help you support how their writing should be presented.

The Key Stage 3 National Strategy Framework for teaching English (DfEE 2001a) divides the writing that students are required to study in English into four categories. These categories make an extremely good starting point in helping you to recognise writing purposes. They are not only useful for English but also as a framework for writing across all subject areas:

1. writing to imagine, explore and entertain;
2. writing to inform, explain and describe;
3. writing to persuade, argue and advise;
4. writing to analyse, review and comment.

Think about a writing task that you have recently supported some students with, if possible outside English. Discuss it with your teaching assistant colleagues. Can you put it into one of the categories above? You may discover that often the writing task fits into more than one category. For example, a newspaper report is there to 'inform', but it also has to 'entertain' us, otherwise we would not read it, and in many articles there is also an attempt to 'persuade' us. However, in general you can usually identify the main purpose of an academic writing task.

Audience

In addition to a purpose, each writing task has a particular audience. Again, students need to think beyond the teacher who is marking their written work as being the audience. It is very important to think carefully about the audience as well as the purpose as this will change the way the work is written. For example, a task may have been to write a piece of work describing the 'Big Bang Theory'. The purpose of this is clearly an information text, which will also explain and describe. However, the writing could be designed for a book to interest eight-year-olds, or it could be to discuss the latest theories in a scientific magazine. Although the purpose is the same, these different audiences will change the writing, as can be seen below.

Structure

Once you have examined the purpose and the audience you can now look at the structure of the writing. Let us look in detail at the 'Big Bang Theory' as it could be written for the two audiences above. Although they are both information and explanation texts, each would have a very different structure at three levels. These writing levels are known as word level, sentence level and text level, and you may have come across them in literacy training. As we noted at the beginning, writing is rather like conducting an orchestra. Although we separate it out into these three levels, to help plan our work, it all has to come together in harmony, rather like a piece of music.

Word-level work is concerned with our choice of vocabulary as well as our spelling. Can the words be informal or slang, as when written in the style of a teenage problem page letter? Is the choice of words made to invoke an emotional response in you? (During the foot and mouth crisis the government chose to call killing 'culling' and some of the articles written by farmers called killing 'murdering'. Both sides used *emotive* vocabulary.

Sentence-level work looks at how we choose to put our sentences together. For example, some texts, such as instructions, need lots of clear, short sentences. In addition, the sentences in instructions usually start with a verb to help us (*warm* the oven to 160 degrees; *chop* the onion).

Whereas imaginative writing may have lots of very long sentences with several adjectives to help paint a visual picture for the reader: 'Her maid, Lena, closed the floor-length midnight-blue velvet curtains' (Lingard 2000).

Text-level work is concerned with how the entire written assignment looks overall. This would include how the sentences are put into paragraphs or whether columns are used as part of the accepted style. It may be that bullet points would be useful in the writing for clarity.

Newspaper reports may contain quotes from witnesses, or pictures with captions.

Completing a PAS for the Big Bang Theory, a book for eight-year-olds

So what might a PAS look like for the above?

Purpose – to inform explain and describe as well as entertain.
Audience – eight-year-old children, just beginning to read independently.
Structure –

Word level:

■ simple words to keep the reading easy;

■ a few scientific words, perhaps with their pronunciations in brackets;

■ possibly exciting adjectives to help a child imagine something they cannot touch or see.

Sentence level:

■ short, simple sentences, to keep the reading easy;

■ perhaps some rhetorical questions to involve the child – 'Have you ever wondered how the Earth began?'

Text level:

■ shiny, robust paper or hardback book;

■ lots of pictures, in colour;

■ small chunks of text, broken up by the pictures;

■ small amount of text on each page;

■ use of a glossary for the few scientific words;

■ use of colour, bold and italics, drawing attention to important points.

Completing a PAS for the 'Big Bang Theory' in a scientific magazine

Purpose – to inform and explain possibly new information but no entertainment value.

Audience – interested scientists with an assumed level of knowledge.

Structure –

Word level:

■ technical vocabulary;

■ scientific vocabulary;

■ large multi-syllabic words.

Sentence level:

■ long, complex sentences with clauses and sub clauses.

Text level:

■ use of an abstract at the beginning;

- written in columns in the style of a magazine article;
- graphs and data plus black-and-white photographs which need a high level of skill to interpret.

You can begin to see that when we ask students to write we are expecting several skills at once. You can also see that by analysing the task, using PAS before starting to write, planning becomes easier. It may be that teachers in your English department use a different *mnemonic*. Find out what it is and use that for your students. This will help them to transfer learning between subjects.

Additionally, teachers often adapt written tasks to make them more stimulating for their students to complete. For example, they may wish to ensure that their students understand what life was like in Roman Britain. However, rather than just asking for a piece of text that informs and describes this they may ask the student to 'imagine you are a Roman soldier and write a letter home to your mother describing what is happening and how you are feeling'. This has now made the written task more interesting, but also more difficult. You can see that it is the purpose of the writing *together* with the audience that will dictate the structure of the writing.

In the appendices to this chapter you will find a useful reminder of the PAS mnemonic to photocopy and use (Appendix 4.1).

Brainstorming and planning ideas for essays, using techniques to match students' preferred learning styles

Students seem to hate the idea of planning essays and written work. You will often hear them say that they do not know where to start a piece of writing. So persuading them of the value of planning is very important. One reason they find this difficult is that they try to brainstorm and sequence their planning in one step. This is difficult; our brains do not always think linearly, ideas jump around and one thought leads to another. Brainstorming first – putting down all of our ideas, whether they are relevant or irrelevant, and in the order they occur to us – needs to be the first step in the extended writing process. It also allows students to use their preferred learning style.

Brainstorming and planning using post-it notes

This technique is useful for both visual and kinaesthetic learners. It works particularly well for writing that has to give a balanced argument, but equally well for other writing. Students use a piece of A3 paper and write the essay title in the middle or the top. Using different coloured 'post it' notes, individual ideas to be included in the essay are written on each note and stuck on to the A3 sheet. As they can be pulled off and moved around the A3 paper easily, students can manipulate their ideas both visually and kinaesthetically. Less confident writers also feel secure, since ideas that are later rejected can be taken off easily and thrown away. In the example below, post-it notes were first used to brainstorm a GCSE coursework essay on *Romeo and Juliet*, the title being 'Who or what do you think was responsible for the young lovers' deaths?'.

As part of their coursework the students had already been given a plan that suggested they look at the following headings: fate, chance, the passion of youth, the fathers (patriarchal society) and other reasons. Each heading was put on to the A3 paper using a different coloured post-it note. As possible reasons for Romeo and Juliet's death were brainstormed they were linked to the headings and written on the appropriate coloured post-it note. They were then stuck together in groups on the paper. One student's personal ideas soon emerged; she had more post-it notes under her headings 'Youthful Passion' and 'Other Reasons' (in particular two adults whom she felt should have known better, the Nurse and the Friar). Still in the brainstorming stage she now went back to her text and selected quotations to back up each of her points. Using her colour coding she stuck these on her sheet.

This post-it method can easily be moved on to the next stage, that of planning the writing sequence. The post-it notes can now be rearranged in a more linear fashion. Having decided that the main argument of the essay was the two reasons noted above, the other reasons are discussed first. So the post-it notes are now ordered with the main arguments left to be discussed in detail last, just before the conclusion. This helps to persuade the reader of your point of view. In this example, the Post-it notes were reordered to discuss the reasons in the following order:

Introduction
Fate
Chance
Fathers and a girl's place in society in Verona
The passion of youth
Poor adult support around the two lovers, the Nurse and the Friar
Conclusion

This method works well for coursework and extended pieces of writing where there is plenty of time for the planning process. It is a method that transfers easily between subjects and writing types. It is also a method that students can use independently but clearly relies on having access to the materials. It is less useful for transferring to exam skills.

Brainstorming using spidergrams and mind maps

Spidergrams are useful for right-brain and visual learners. They also encourage the use of *key words*, which can be used later to plan the key sentences of the writing. Spidergrams allow you to write the main heading in the centre of a page. The ideas to be included in the writing are then written on lines radiating from the centre, rather like the legs of a spider. If each leg is reduced to key words, rather than a long sentence, this can help focus the planning. Students find it very difficult to write just using key words, but try to encourage this. It links to what is discussed in Chapter 3 on note-taking. Reading and writing are opposite processes. Therefore if in reading paragraphs are reduced to key sentences and then further to key words, in writing key words can be used to write key sentences and then paragraphs. Remembering that writing and reading are opposite processes is useful; it allows you to point out good examples and to use some of their reading as models for their own writing.

Spidergrams are *not* simple mind maps. Mind maps organise information, with the most important information being on large branches and less important but connected information being added to smaller branches off the same branch. Initially, spidergrams do not have the information ordered or sequenced. However, you will find many people who confuse the terminology of spidergrams with mind maps.

Once the brainstorm has been completed as a spidergram it will need to be organised to become the writing plan. This can be achieved in two ways. First, numbers can be added to each leg to form the key words for each paragraph, sentence or topic to be covered, as shown in the example below, a geography homework at Key Stage 3 on 'extinction'.

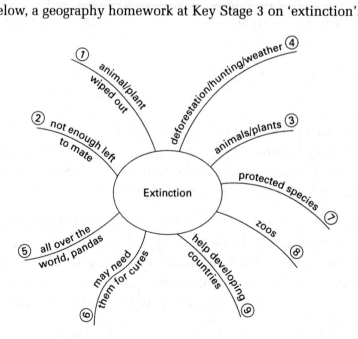

Figure 4.1 *Spidergram on extinction*

The above method is quick and easy but cannot deal with planning complex writing tasks. Secondly, for large pieces of extended writing the spidergram can be redrawn as a mind map. The information from different legs can be collected together to form main headings for branches. Additional, related, information can be added to these branches as sub-branches. There are several books, software programs, videos and tapes available to teach mind mapping so it is not discussed in detail within this book, but you should be aware of the differences between spidergrams and mind maps. Suitable references are available in Chapter 5.

Brainstorming and planning using 'linear methods'

Many students – particularly left-brain, logical thinkers and those who are auditory learners – feel uncomfortable with the above methods and prefer their initial brainstorm to have a line-like (linear) structure that resembles a list. However, this can still be completed in two phases, the brainstorm and then the planning.

Bullet points

Ideas to be included are brainstormed as bullet points in a list. Each bullet point is reduced to a key word or words. Once all bullet points have been brainstormed they can then be grouped together as themes emerge. This can be done by highlighting all those that are linked in separate colours. Finally, once the bullet points are highlighted and grouped they can be numbered in the order in which the student wants to write about them within their work. Less confident students can conduct this process on mini whiteboards and can then copy it onto paper once the plan has emerged. The example in Figure 4.2 is a bullet point brainstorm and plan for a discursive essay 'Should vending machines be allowed in schools?'. A copy for use can be found in Appendix 4.3.

The six Ws (Appendix 4.2)

As was noted earlier in this chapter, reading and writing are opposites of the same process and so the six Ws are also discussed in Chapter 3. Very often, using the six W words 'who', 'what', 'where', 'when', 'why' and 'how' can form a useful brainstorm and planning point for the start of a piece of writing. This can initially use a writing frame for support, but providing students can remember the six W words this method can be relied upon easily without any frame and transfers to many non-fiction writing tasks. Below is an example of the same homework as above, on extinction, planned using the six Ws (Figure 4.3). You will see that the writing frame has numbers in the circles. The numbers were added after the initial brainstorm in order to

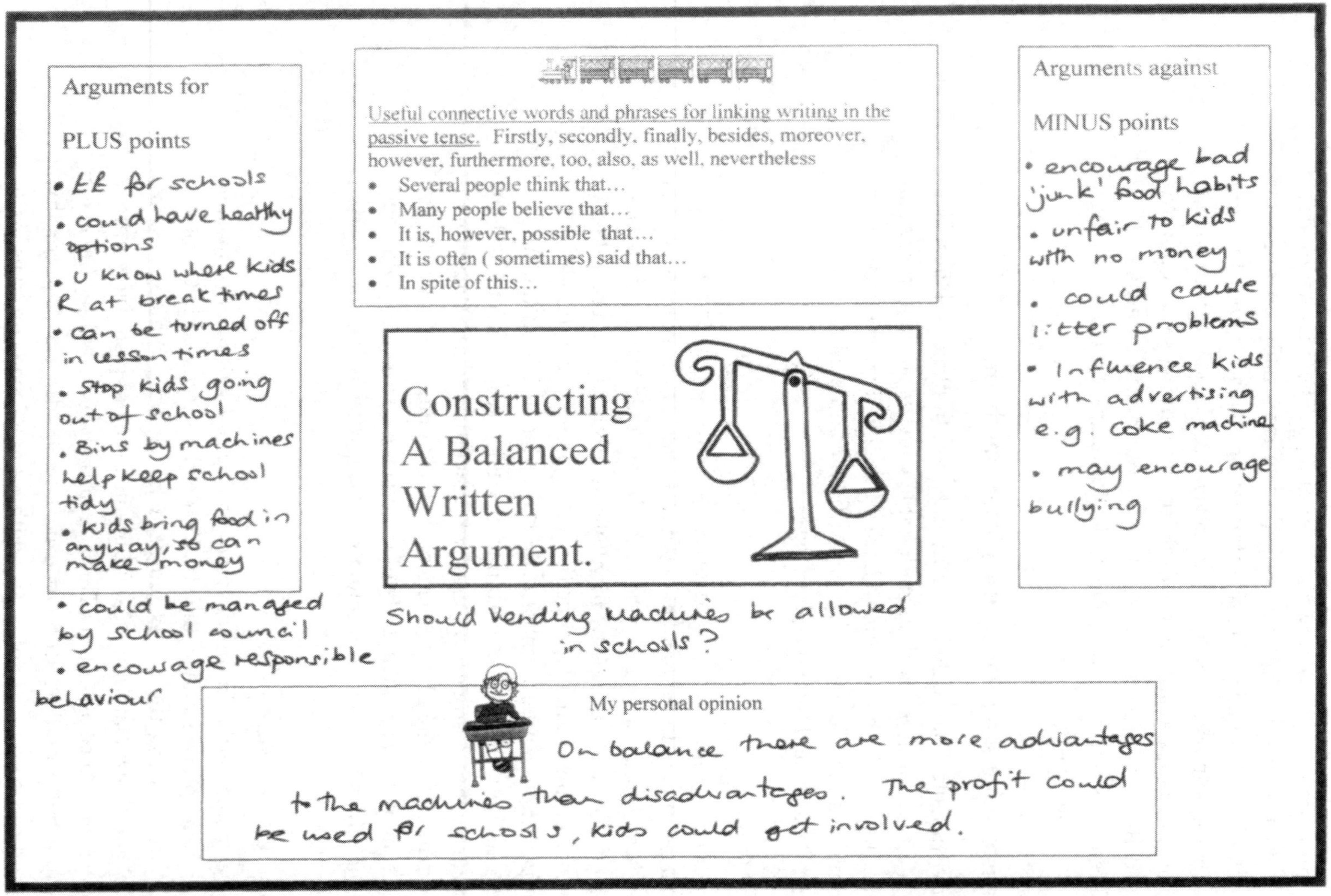

Constructing A Balanced Written Argument.

Arguments for

PLUS points
- ££ for schools
- could have healthy options
- U know where kids R at break time
- Can be turned off in lesson times
- stop kids going out of school
- Bins by machines help keep school tidy
- kids bring food in anyway, so can make money
- could be managed by school council
- encourage responsible behaviour

Arguments against

MINUS points
- encourage bad 'junk' food habits
- unfair to kids with no money
- could cause litter problems
- Influence kids with advertising e.g. Coke machine
- may encourage bullying

Useful connective words and phrases for linking writing in the passive tense. Firstly, secondly, finally, besides, moreover, however, furthermore, too, also, as well, nevertheless
- Several people think that…
- Many people believe that…
- It is, however, possible that…
- It is often (sometimes) said that…
- In spite of this…

Should Vending machines be allowed in schools?

My personal opinion

On balance there are more advantages than disadvantages. The profit could to the machines be used for schools, kids could get involved.

Figure 4.2 Vending machine essay plan

sequence the writing. Additionally, the 'who' was crossed out, as it was not important for the *purpose* of this writing assignment, which was an information and explanation text. (In a history assignment the 'who' may be the most important W as part of the writing purpose.)

The hamburger

This method seems to suit all learning styles, as it has elements of visual, kinaesthetic and auditory learning. I have chosen to put it within the linear discussion as the hamburger tends to order the brainstorm. Initially, you can use large A4 pictures of hamburgers from clip art software, or draw your own.

Once students can 'visualise' the hamburgers you no longer need them as pictures for their planning. The idea of the hamburger is that the split bread roll at the top and the bottom help to hold the writing together, like the introduction and conclusion in an essay, or the title of a scientific investigation and its concluding findings. The inside of the hamburger then contains the 'meat' of the writing. This allows you to have a very simple hamburger, where there are only a few ideas inside, or a 'mega burger', with lots of layers to give a very detailed piece of writing. The hamburger is split apart and each layer is brainstormed. Once brainstormed, the layers are then reassembled in the order the student wishes to use them. Below are two hamburger plans for a short piece of writing, followed by the students' first draft and final copy. The purpose was to write a speech persuading tourists. Students could choose whether to write to persuade tourists to buy some snake skins in the tourist market or not to buy them. You will note that both of these students had successfully carried out a PAS too, since their writing structure fits the purpose and the audience well.

Writing frames

A discussion of brainstorming and planning would not be complete without looking at writing frames. There are several published writing frames available. You have also been provided with two within this chapter (Appendix 4.2, The six Ws, and an additional Appendix 4.3 for use with discursive essay writing). Writing frames have strengths and weaknesses.

So what are writing frames? 'Writing frames are templates consisting of starters, connectives and sentence modifiers which offer children a structure for communicating what they want to say' (Lewis and Wray 1998). They have advantages and disadvantages.

Advantages:

■ They offer structure to those students whose written organisational skills are lacking.

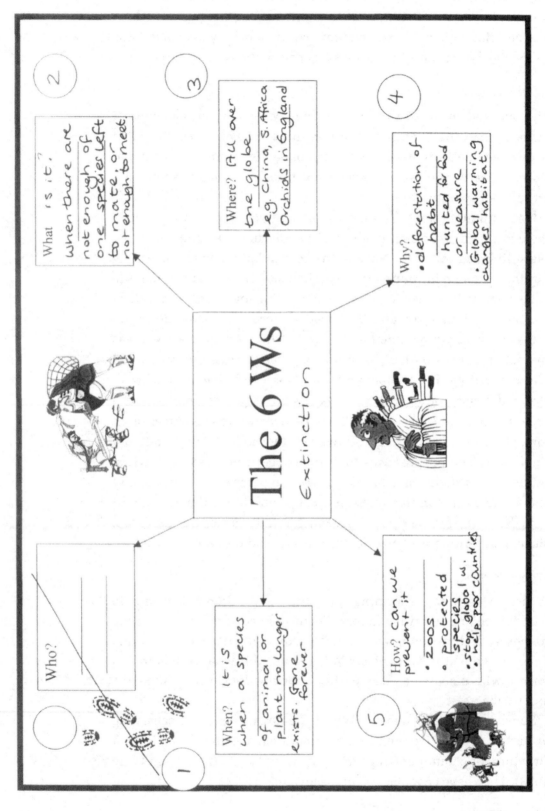

The 6 Ws

Extinction

① When? It is
when a species
of animal or
plant no longer
exists. Gone
forever

② What is it?
When there are
not enough of
one species left
to mate, or
not enough to meet

③ Where? All over
the globe
e.g. China, S. Africa
Orchids in England

④ Why?
• deforestation of
habitat
• hunted for food
or pleasure
• Global warming
changes habitat

⑤ How? can we
prevent it
• zoos
• protected
species
• stop global w.
• help poor countries

Who?

Figure 4.3 *Six Ws plan for extinction essay*

Figure 4.4 *The 'hamburger'*

- They can save a student from 'freezing' and not knowing how to start.
- They develop appropriate formal language and use of connectives.
- They encourage a student to write using paragraphs.
- They show students that differing text types require different writing styles, thus reinforcing purpose, audience and style.

Disadvantages:

- They can constrain a student's writing style.
- If introduced without appropriate teacher modelling and support they are unsuccessful and can become yet another thing that a student has failed at. They are often given to students without this important stage.
- Unless carefully used, the student becomes over-dependent on writing frames and in examination situations is unlikely to be able to plan and write effectively.
- They can discourage *metacognition*.

From plan to pen and paper

So now your students have a good plan. However, it is only a few key words, carefully sequenced, and it has got to become an extended essay, perhaps over 1000 words. This section deals with how to extend the plan to produce the end result.

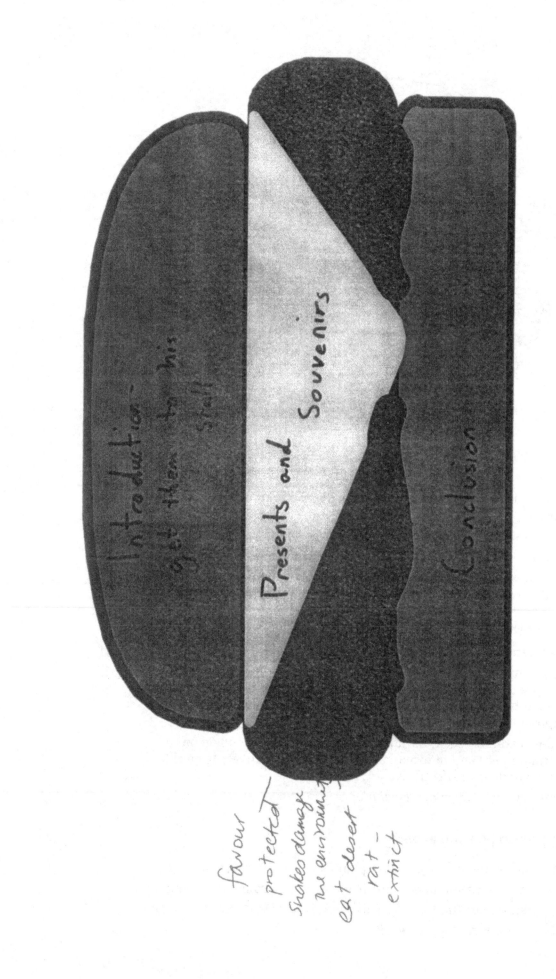

Figure 4.5(a) *Burger plan (Pupil 1)*

"Hello Madame would you be interested where do you come from?" Askes the spop can I invite you to my special stall you I garuntie that you'll see some things that you never seen before. Theres no other stall like mine. Mino will sell you aa genuine | 12 foot long python skin. Its just g down here.

Novelties

This snake skin would make brilliont present or souviear. Every time you look at it you'll see remember this fantastic holiday. Any one that you give this to I guarantee they will have noth like it.

If you are worried about damaging the environment, dont be. Africa is over run with snakes, sf theres far to many of them Attttt, you'll be helping the environment. The pythons are killing the desert rat which is becoming nea extintion. So by purchaing a python you'll be protecting a rat.

Consequently holiday makers I can offer you such a brilliant price. You would think that this would be 200 american dolars but no its only 150 but to you $ 125 $. Do I have any offers, who could resist such a bargin.

Worrie

worry   worried

Figure 4.5(b) *First draft (Pupil 1)*

An extended piece of writing should follow the rules below:

1. Tell your reader what you are *going* to say (the *introduction*).
2. Say it (the main body of your writing; the ideas of which you have already planned and sequenced).
3. Remind them what you have said (the conclusion).

The rules work equally well with extended design and technology briefs:

1. Tell your reader what the design brief is.
2. Write about your research, ideas, the modifications to meet the brief as it emerged, and your design.
3. Evaluate how effectively you met the brief.

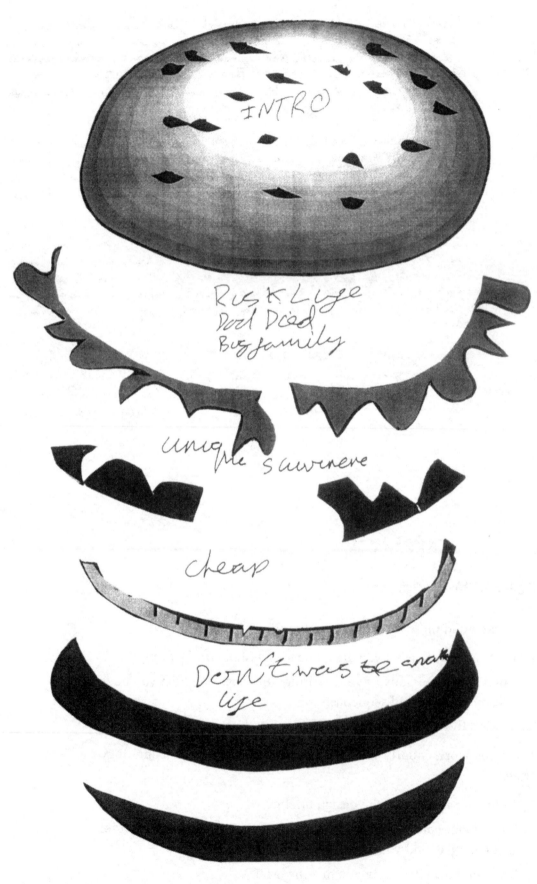

Figure 4.6(a) *Burger plan*

Hello people of Africa if you want to go
home and have something your friend would
envy look at this — a beautiful snake skin

My dad I risked my life for this one
of a kind snake skin. I could have lost
my life for your luxury. My dad did doing
this job but asked me to carry on the business
. Look I have a big family and they all need
feeding so please buy this wonderful snakeskin. And and put a meat on my familys plates
tonight, please!

Bring back a unique souvenir for your friends,
next door neibours or anyone else to
envy over. Have the one thing that know one
else has.

Buy this golden brown yellowy jet
Python skin it would would look even better
above your fire place wouldn't it? But maybe
you don't want it there you could have have
it as a hadbag or hat or any other type of clothing

Figure 4.6(b) *First handwritten draft*

Why buy my snake skin?

Hello, madam, where do you come from? Can I invite you to my spectacular stall? I guarantee that you'll see some novelties you've never seen before. There's no other stall like mine. Mine will sell you a genuine 12-foot snakeskin. It's just down here.

This snakeskin would make a brilliant present or souvenir. Every time you look at it you'll remember this fantastic holiday. Anyone that you give this to will have nothing like it. This snakeskin will be the envy of all your friends.

If you are worried about damaging the environment, don't be; Africa is overrun with snakes; in fact there's far too many of them. You'll be helping the environment. The pythons are killing the desert rat, which is near to extinction. So by purchasing a python you'll be protecting a rat.

Consequently, I can offer holiday-makers a brilliant price. You would think that this would be 200 American dollars, but no, it is only 150 dollars, but to you 125 dollars. Do I have any offers? Who could resist such a bargain?

Figure 4.7 *Final copy*

Writing effective paragraphs

As was noted in Chapter 3, all good paragraphs start with a key sentence, sometimes referred to as a *power sentence*. These sentences guide the structure of the writing. They should be reasonably short sentences. They must include the key word from your plan. Some students prefer to prepare ahead so plan and write all of their key sentences for each paragraph before they start writing in full. Other students prefer to think about each key sentence from their key word in the plan as they progress through the essay and begin each paragraph. Neither approach is wrong; again, it depends on a student's preferred learning style. However, whichever way they choose it should be possible, when they have finished it, to go through their essay and highlight the key sentence at the beginning of each paragraph and to get a good idea of the contents of the writing. It is exactly the same principle as when they were taught to take notes in Chapter 3. Below are the power sentences for the students' extended piece of writing on the *Romeo and Juliet* essay discussed above.

Why did Romeo and Juliet die?

Many people have different views on why Romeo and Juliet died, some say it was fate, others say it was chance, or even the feud between the two families. However, people have even come to believe it was the fathers, or adolescent passion. Yet others have come to other conclusions, and I am going to investigate each aspect and come to my own conclusion for the death of Romeo and Juliet.

- Fate: could it have been fate, 'written in the stars', as they say, that may have caused the young lovers' deaths?
- Was it chance that caused their deaths?
- The feud between the two households is a possibility why Romeo and Juliet died.
- Was it the fathers that caused the deaths of both Romeo and Juliet? It may have been the fact that Verona's male-dominated society was responsible for their deaths.
- Even though I have found evidence that Romeo and Juliet may have died because of fate, chance or the feud and their fathers, I think that there are other more important reasons behind their deaths.
- I have found enough evidence to lead me to believe their deaths could have been as a result of adolescent passion.
- In addition, I think it also could have been through the fault of certain adults' irrational behaviour.
- The lovers are fated to die, as we know from the opening lines of the play.

Once the power sentence has been written the rest of the paragraph must only contain information related to that paragraph. It seems obvious, and if you ask students the rules for when to start a new paragraph they can tell you the correct answer. But they do not always put this into practice.

One way of supporting the development of each paragraph following the key sentence is the use of a mnemonic (see Chapter 5). This mnemonic is: SIEGE. The SI stands for SAY IT; that is, write your key sentence. The E stands for EXPLAIN; that is, explain what you mean in your key sentence. The G stands for GIVE an example. In an English essay this may be a quotation. In a science write up this may be to describe in detail the reaction you saw. In a geography essay this may mean to cite a particular case study example (for example, when discussing earthquakes, using the facts from the Kobe earthquake). The E stands for EVALUATE it. This is where the student has an opportunity to look back at the writing title and relate their own point of view and analyse the value of the point they are making. It is the highest order thinking part (see Chapter 3) and is where you gain the highest grades. It ensures that you **keep answering the question**. This may sound simple, but lots of students lose marks for writing *irrelevant* information. In simpler writing the E is not always necessary. Below is an example of the SIEGE paragraphing technique used in the student's *Romeo and Juliet* essay.

> The feud between the two households is a possibility why Romeo and Juliet died. The Montagues and the Capulets are rival enemies 'ancient grudge breaks to new mutiny' and for Romeo a Montague and Juliet a Capulet they would never have been allowed to associate especially not love one another. So for these two people they had no other choice than to keep their love affair a secret. Juliet finds Romeo that bit more attractive because he is a Montague and vice versa and it is not allowed so she finds the whole love affair exciting. When Juliet walks about the orchard she expresses her feelings with one of the most famous lines in Romeo and Juliet 'Romeo Romeo wherefore art thou Romeo?' Here she is saying Romeo why are you Romeo why do you have to be Montague. This shows how the feud is in the way of Juliet's love for Romeo. If Romeo and Juliet could talk to their parents about their love then they wouldn't have had to get married in secret and hide their love, the friar then agrees because he thinks it may lead to a reconciliation between the opposing families. If the families were at least at peace with one another then Romeo would never have killed Tybalt. When Juliet's father arranged for Juliet to marry Paris, if there was no feud Juliet would have been able to tell her father she was in love with Romeo, and wanted to marry him. Moreover if the families were at peace then Juliet would never have been in such a panic for an escape plan and agreed to Friar Lawrence's plan. Then Juliet and Romeo would never have killed themselves they would have talked to their parents.

Clearly not all writing types will be supported by the use of this order, but many analytical, discursive and persuasive writing types will be. It is of benefit because the student remains focused on the paragraph content and does not stray into discussing other ideas. Not all students can remember mnemonics either. But the basic principle can be supported without the use of this mnemonic (SIEGE).

Drafting and redrafting

I have yet to find a student, or an adult, that enjoys the drafting and redrafting process. Yet it must be done. The last section in this chapter deals with *active* ways of checking and improving written work. Helping students redraft their work involves giving good oral feedback as well as sharing the skills for them to use independently. Whilst these chapters can be read in isolation, it would be useful to read the section on the 'Feedback Sandwich' in Chapter 2.

It was noted at the beginning of this chapter that writing is rather like conducting an orchestra – lots of tasks have to come together in a process known as multi-tasking. Some students have the ability to do this well. They have a good *working memory* (discussed in detail in Chapter 5). However, many students have less effective working memories and find it difficult to do everything at once. They can sequence the writing well, but the spelling 'goes'. They will spell accurately and write legibly, but at the expense of the sentence construction, and they will miss words out. For most students this means that all written work needs to be checked through and improved or redrafted before handing in.

Active methods of checking work

If you ask most students if they have checked their work they usually say they have read through it. This is passive. Active methods involve 'doing' something with the writing. One way of supporting such skills is to separate draft checking into two separate skills to check: *secretarial skills* and *authorial skills*.

Secretarial skills

These include checking the following:

- Spelling
- Punctuation
- Defining paragraphs appropriately, i.e. using indentation with handwritten work, as is some schools' policy, or missing out a line if using a word processor.

The word processor has now made this job much easier. For handwritten work active strategies still need to be employed.

1. For spelling: take a highlighter pen and start at the *bottom* of the work checking backwards to the top. As no meaning can be gained,

the eye is forced to see each word, exactly as it is written; otherwise it reads what you wanted to write. If students never have any spelling errors it may be that they are choosing vocabulary that they can spell, rather than vocabulary that expresses what they want to say more effectively. This is known as 'staying in the safety zone'. Apart from the lucky few who are naturally good spellers, there should always be some spelling errors, as we continually strive to choose a richer vocabulary for our written work.

2. English is full of *homophones*. These are words that sound the same but are spelt differently, such as 'their' and 'there'. These are not spelling mistakes. If the same ones keep occurring students need to find a way of sorting their own 'pet hates' out. Homophones need to be checked by reading from the beginning of the work to the end.

3. For punctuation take a different highlighter pen. Students should read the work from the beginning to the end *out loud*. Read every word slowly, checking that no words have been missed out. As the work is read aloud check that the punctuation used is helpful. (Apart from a few interested intellectuals, punctuation is not an exact science, but it should help the reader.) Would an extra comma be useful? Is that sentence far too long; could it be split up into two separate sentences? Do the words 'then', 'and' or 'next' keep appearing so that the paragraph is just one big long sentence? If possible, students should use a 'study buddy' or 'critical friend' to read their work for them. It is always difficult to find your own sec-retarial mistakes, but a study buddy will usually spot them immediately because the work is not within their head, it is just on the page.

Authorial skills

Authorial skills are concerned with the content of the written work and its style. This is perhaps the area that students are less aware of when draft checking their work and is an excellent starting point for constructive criticism using the feedback sandwich. You can use the foundations of PAS to check the work for authorial skills.

1. The work needs to be checked for meaning. This can be completed while the work is being read out loud for punctuation. Very often students fail to write essential details in their work because they assume that since their audience is the teacher they do not need to. After all, she or he already knows about it. This chapter has shown that the audience is not the teacher. The content of the work must be able to stand alone, without any assumptions about the readers' knowledge. It is useful to be able to say to students, 'If you do not

show evidence in your writing to the examiner or the teacher that you know about something, they cannot give you marks for it. Never assume that they know that you know.'

2. Check the use of vocabulary. Most students' work can be improved significantly by careful choice of more precise language. Encourage students to select at least three vocabulary changes to improve their work. They do not have to use a thesaurus if they do not wish to. Most students have an in-built thesaurus, and just need to be encouraged to use it. A carefully chosen word, incorrectly spelt, will be much better than a correctly spelt, weaker word. For example, 'The rabbit comes out of its burrow in the early evening' is much better when rewritten as, 'The rabbit emerges from its burrow at dusk'.

3. Is the choice of words suitable for the purpose of the writing, the audience and the style? Look at the example below, and note how the mood of the writing is changed by the selection of the verbs. The first example is a neutral text; the second changes the mood to a positive one, and the last to a negative one. As we have noted, neither is wrong; the words need to suit the audience and the purpose.

4. Check the sequencing of the writing. For most non-fiction essays you should be able to take a highlighter pen and highlight the first sentence in each paragraph. When read aloud, these should give you the main points of the writing, i.e. they should be the *power sentences*.

5. Check that the writing flows. Have connectives been used well to help the writing flow? Connectives are additional words that bring the sentences in a paragraph together, such as 'however', 'in addition', 'firstly', 'secondly' and 'finally'. Connectives also help to introduce subsequent paragraphs, connecting them to the previous

---

The boy <u>went</u> down the lane. As he <u>got</u> to the field he listened to the <u>sound</u> of the birds and <u>said</u>, 'What a <u>smell</u> the hedgerow has today'.

The boy <u>skipped</u> down the lane. As he <u>reached</u> the field he listened to the <u>melody</u> of the birds and <u>sighed</u>, 'What a lovely <u>scent</u> the hedgerow has today'.

The boy <u>sneaked</u> down the lane. As he <u>skirted</u> the field he listened to the <u>cacophony</u> of the birds and <u>retorted</u>, 'What a <u>stench</u> the hedgerow has today'.

Figure 4.8 *Choosing vocabulary carefully*

one. The Key Stage 3 *Literacy Across the Curriculum Folder* provides a list of useful connectives. You will also note that there are some examples of connectives on the Balanced Argument writing frame within this chapter (Figure 4.2).

Summary

Writing is a complex skill, which requires practice and feedback. This chapter has discussed several aspects of students' writing. Use careful target setting and feedback to support students in improving their written work using a staged approach as noted in Chapter 2.

End-of-chapter checklist (tick when achieved)

☐ I can use PAS or the school's mnemonic to help plan writing.

☐ I understand the writing needs to be planned at the word, sentence and text level.

☐ I have used the six Ws.

☐ I have used spidergrams.

☐ I have used mind maps.

☐ I have used post-it notes.

☐ I have used bullet points and key words.

☐ I have used the balanced argument writing frame.

☐ I have used the hamburger method.

☐ I understand how to support writing power sentences using key words.

☐ I understand how to write a paragraph using SIEGE or the school's preferred method.

☐ I know what authorial skills are and can support their improvement.

☐ I know what secretarial skills are and can use active strategies to improve them with students.

5 Managing memory skills

Chapter overview

To be successful within the education system students have to demonstrate: knowledge – for example remembering facts; understanding – such as interpreting tables and information; and skills – including essay writing techniques. Having an efficient memory will therefore have a significant impact on these and, in particular, on knowledge-based skills. Whilst individuals may differ in their capacity to remember things (or in their own perception of how good their memory is) there are several skills and techniques that students can be taught to make the most efficient use of the memory they have.

By the end of this chapter you will be able to support students in managing their memory by:

■ having a brief understanding of long- and short-term memory;

■ having several active strategies to aid revision and recall including:

　1. using the number peg system to remember sequenced information;
　2. making mnemonics to help recall facts;
　3. using storytelling to remember sequenced information; and
　4. reducing information for revision using mind maps.

Some useful terminology

The link between the brain, as a physical organ, and how the mind works is still one that we know very little about. Years ago the only way to investigate the brain was to wait and examine it after serious injury or death. For example, autopsies on people who had had dyslexia revealed differences in the right half and the left half of the brain when compared to non-dyslexic individuals. However, with recent technological developments it is now possible to study the brain in action in living individuals. Although this has led to a greater understanding of how our memory works, we are still a long way from fully understanding this wonderful organ that, as human beings, sets us apart from other animals. As a teaching assistant it is useful to have some understanding of the theoretical terminology related to memory. It will help you to understand some of the learning behaviours that you observe every day within the classroom, and provide you with suitable strategies to support them.

Short-term memory

This is where a small amount of material is held in the mind over a period of several seconds only. It is described as involving *primary memory* if the material is held passively and then given back as a response in the same form. For example, asking someone to repeat the instructions you have just given them involves the short-term memory.

Working memory

This is, perhaps, more important to understand. This is where a small amount of material is held in the short-term memory *and* must be mixed and/or reorganised with either more incoming information or with information already learned. You will often observe poor working memory in students. One example would be in completing long mathematical problems as they progress towards GCSE. They may get half way through the problem and then forget what they were doing and why they were doing that particular small part of the problem in order to get to the answer, i.e. the mixing and reorganising of the information is too much for the working memory to cope with. Different students have varying working memory capacities and a poor working memory makes many life skills difficult. Students with dyslexia have poor working memory skills, but there are lots of students in classrooms who may experience working memory difficulties.

Semantic memory

When we learn new words we need to store them in the brain so that we can *retrieve* them from our long-term memory when we need to use them again. Our semantic memory is linked to the *meaning* of the word. We need to know what the new word means and have links to other connected words in order to store it away efficiently. If you shadow a Year 7 class throughout one school day you will be amazed at the amount of new language that is introduced. Each new word needs to be discussed and *linked with words they already know* so that it can be stored away correctly. You can help by providing the memory hooks. For example, they may need to be able to learn and use the word 'delta'. This would need to be linked semantically to words such as river, flood and silt. It is more likely that they would already know the words 'river' and 'flood', so this would be the starting point for its semantic storage.

Phonological awareness

This is a person's ability to analyse the sound system of the language they use. For example, if I write the word 'clud', which is not a real word, you would still be able to read it, since you have phonological awareness and can analyse the sound system of your own language. We also use this phonic knowledge to store new words. So new words are stored and retrieved by sound, as well as by meaning. You will probably have experienced this when you are tired and are searching in your mind for the name of a place, or a word you wish to use in conversation. You may say to someone, 'Oh, I know it, it begins with 'p'!', and eventually the word surfaces and you were usually correct about the initial sound or the rhyme in the word. Storing words phonically is something we all do. Some students have much less efficient phonological awareness, and will store most of their words using semantics (meaning). Others who have good phonological awareness will use the sounds of the words to store them away. This means that students need to be able to hear how the new vocabulary is pronounced *at the same time* as they see the word on the whiteboard or in the text, before it can be stored away efficiently. You will be able to observe the pupils who are your 'semantic storers'; they will often read or use a word that has a similar meaning to the one they should be using. For example, young children may read 'leg' as 'foot'; older students may read 'element' for 'compound'.

To ensure new vocabulary is stored away well, expect students to begin using new vocabulary in context, orally, straight away.

Auditory sequential memory

This is the ability to recall, in a particular order, groups of words, telephone numbers, facts, oral instructions given by the teacher, days of the week, months of the year and multiplication tables. Again, we all have varied abilities in this area, but students who cannot remember their times tables are also likely to be the ones who cannot remember all of the above.

Visual memory

This is the ability to recall or retain a *mental picture* of a letter, word or object including its shape, length and order of letters.

Processing speed

Processing speed can be viewed as the equivalent of the gigahertz in a computer. For example, a 'Pentium 3' chip can process more at the same time than a 'Pentium 2' because it works faster. It is no more accurate; it is just faster. Processing speed is the speed at which the brain can work. Some students may have up to 27 per cent smaller processing systems in the brain. This does not mean that they cannot remember, retrieve or manipulate information, but that their system works more slowly. This has implications for you as the teaching assistant. Do not always provide answers until you have given a student sufficient time to 'find' them for him/herself. When working with groups of students you must be very strict about not allowing students to butt in when others are being asked for a response. Otherwise students with slow processing speeds eventually give up, as they know someone will shout out the answer before they have had time to think about it themselves. This, in turn, means that their processing speed becomes even slower.

Therefore, give some students extra time to retrieve information from their long-term memory before expecting an answer. Ask the question and say that you will return for the answer in a minute. Meanwhile ask someone else a question.

Students with poor working and short-term memories have difficulty multi-tasking. Do not sit them near students who find this easy. These include those that can chat *and* work versus those that can chat *or* work.

Active strategies to aid revision and recall

There are three main areas related to managing memory skills: putting knowledge and skills into the memory store; ensuring they remain in the store; and retrieving them for use out of the store.

Putting it into the store

We have already noted that new ideas, concepts and vocabulary are stored by meaning and sound and that all students will use their strengths to store new words rather than their weaknesses.

You can help the storage of new vocabulary in several ways:

- Always ensure students have a list of key subject-specific words for a topic that they understand. Most subject departments have topic keyword lists. You may need to add a familiar word beside each key word to aid the semantic link. Don't turn the exercise into a spelling one; many words that are needed for meaning will not need to be spelled. This is particularly the case for exam skills and will be returned to in Chapter 6.

■ Create visual images and families to help storage. For example, the Triangle Family all live together as one big, happy, but strange, family (Figure 5.1). QUEEN ISOSCELES is beautiful; she is tall and slim; whereas happy KING EQUILATERAL is short and plump. Their daughter, PRINCESS RIGHT ANGLE, is very lazy, she spends her time propped up against the wall reading a book, with her legs stuck out, which everyone trips over. She owns a strange alien dog from outer space who can change shape. She calls him SCALENE.

■ We have already discussed linking visual images to the meaning of words. If using the word 'chronology', draw clock faces in the 'o's. Turn the letter 'o's in the word chlorophyll into leaves and write the word in green.

Keeping it in the store

It is a sad fact that you will be unable to recall 80 per cent of this chapter within 24 hours of having read it (Buzan 1989). This is the same for everyone. It is essential that in order to keep something active within your memory it will need to be reviewed. Many students, when they come to revise for an exam, find that they have forgotten everything and are re-learning the entire syllabus again. Reviewing learning is an essential study skill, particularly during revision periods in the lead up to exams. Planning a review timetable will be discussed in detail in Chapter 6.

Similarly, during a lesson, students are most likely to remember what was covered at the beginning and the end of the session and forget the middle portion. This is why teachers spend time at the beginning of a lesson explaining the aims of the lesson and then return at the end of the lesson to review what has been covered. (This is often referred to as the plenary.)

Getting it out of the store

There are several techniques, or tools, for supporting students' memories and retrieving information. As a teaching assistant you need to be aware of as many of these as possible. Depending on your preferred learning style, and your brain's preferred way of memory storage, some methods will not suit you, but they may suit the students you have to support. It is therefore important to know as many strategies as possible and to begin to know which tools will suit individual students. Each tool needs to be introduced and practised. However, opportunities for trying out the various techniques need to be found when the stakes are not too high. For example, do not try using a new

King Equilateral

Queen Isosceles

Princess Right angle

Her alien dog-scalene

Figure 5.1 *The Triangle Family*

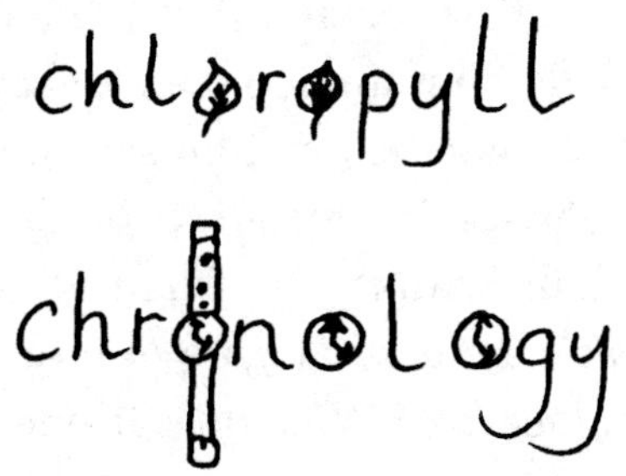

chloropyll

chronology

Figure 5.2 *Linking images*

memory technique for the first time in an end-of-term exam where the results may influence which set the student will be put in the following year. If possible, work with the subject teacher and explain that the students you have been supporting are trying out a new revision method for their end-of-module test.

The number peg system

This is excellent when information has to be remembered in a sequence, but it can also be used to remember key headings for essays in exams. It relies on both visualisation techniques and rhyme. Some students with very poor phonology find it useless, as they cannot remember which item rhymes with which number. First, the numbers 1–10 are linked to objects whose names rhyme with their number but of which it is easy to create visual images within the mind. Students need to learn the items that are rhymed to each of the numbers 1–10 before they can start to use the system. This remains constant for all revision.

1. bun
2. shoe
3. tree
4. door
5. hive
6. sticks
7. heaven
8. gate
9. line/vine/wine (depending on the age of the student – I find 'vine' useless for younger students as they cannot visualise it)
10. hen

Imagine that we have to remember the key factors affecting economic development in Southern Italy to discuss in a geography essay within an exam. There are eight factors: transport, the weather, soil erosion, earthquakes, volcanoes, general poverty, and the factors known in geography as push/pull factors. The first factor is 'transport' or lack of it. The student needs to first recall 1 (bun), then visualise their bun and make a visual link in their mind to the first key word to be remembered, i.e. transport. I visualise a 'Chelsea bun' and to link it to transport I make an image in my mind of the bun with wheels. Students really need help with these visualisation skills. Get them to shut their eyes and ask them what type of bun they are imagining. How big is it? What colour is it? What does it smell like?

The second factor is the weather. Number 2 is rhymed with shoe, so the student needs to link their visual image of a shoe to weather. I visualise a flip-flop, as the weather in Southern Italy is hot. But I have known students who visualise Wellington boots and this works too. The visualisations should be personal, otherwise they do not work. The third factor is erosion. Number 3 is rhymed with tree, so a visual link needs to be made between tree and erosion. I visualise the roots of a tree exposed, with the dry soil blowing around them. Again, you need to be sure they are really painting a visual picture of a tree in their mind. Ask them to shut their eyes and describe it to you. This sequence continues until all items have been memorised. Students need practise at visualising, and should use all of their senses, colour and humour. Negative images will not be remembered as the brain is programmed to forget negative experiences. Some boys need to be persuaded not to use negative or violent images.

Below is my number peg system used for the eight factors affecting poverty in Southern Italy.

1 = bun = poor transport (a Chelsea bun on cartoon wheels)
2 = shoe = weather (a pink flip-flop in the scorching sun)
3 = tree = erosion (a tree with all of the roots exposed, all knotted and dry)
4 = door = earthquakes (a door cracking loudly and sinking into the room as the earth opens up)
5 = hive = volcanoes (add your own image)
6 = sticks = people start off poor (add your own image)
7 = heaven = pull factors towards the rich cities (add your own image)
8 = gate = push factors the drive away from poor rural areas (add your own image)

You may think that students would become muddled if they have lots of different number peg systems for different subjects. This does not seem to happen; and if it does, do not use the method. You may also be tempted to provide pictures of the number pegs for students to help them with this technique. However, they really do need to learn to visualise them personally as an active strategy, so that they adapt each one to the key concept that they are trying to memorise.

Telling a story

An alternative method to the number peg system is to make up a sequenced story. This really suits students who prefer to use their semantic memory. Below is the order of light waves in the spectrum of light. The order needs to be remembered for GCSE Physics.

Radio waves – microwaves – infra-red waves – visible light waves – ultra-violet light waves – x-ray waves and gamma rays

You can make up a story to remember the sequence. For example, it could start as follows:

Early one morning the *radio* alarm woke me with a start. I slipped on my cosy slippers, went downstairs and put my porridge in the *microwave*. While it cooked I plonked myself lazily in the chair and pressed the TV remote to put on the TV. Thank goodness for *infra-red* light … [Can you continue the story?]

While it is more fun if students make up their own story it would be possible to make the story up as a group, or to prepare a story to use with the students you support. It is important that the story flows logically, otherwise the importance of the sequence is lost. Try making up a story for a sequenced topic you have just supported.

Mnemonics

A mnemonic is a word or rhyme that helps you to remember a fact or a spelling. The first letter is used as a memory prompt. You probably use one to recall the colours of the rainbow: Richard of York Gave Battle In Vain – red, orange, yellow, green, blue, indigo, violet. Or perhaps you used them for remembering the order of musical notes that sit in the lines, and between the lines, of a music staff (FACE for the gaps and Every Good Boy Deserves Football for the EBGDF notes on the lines). Used in moderation, mnemonics can be useful. However, some students with word storage difficulties, particularly poor phonology, can remember the mnemonic but forget what word each item is associated with. Therefore try to make the mnemonic meaningful to the subject matter, as below. This is a mnemonic for remembering the order of the planets from the sun:

My **v**ery **e**asy **m**ethod **j**ust **s**peeds **u**p **n**aming **p**lanets.
(Mercury, Venus, Earth, Mars, Jupiter, Saturn, Uranus, Neptune, Pluto)

Mind mapping

So what is mind mapping? It was pioneered by Tony Buzan. It is a way of dealing with information and presenting it to your brain as key concepts in a visual way. Many students find they become overloaded with the vast quantity of text presented in a linear way, such as their

Figure 5.3 *Solar system*

usual notes from the board or a textbook. Mind mapping links key words with colour and visual symbols. It allows creative and spatial skills to work with, and support, language skills, which are reduced to important words and concepts only. Mind mapping can be used for planning essays, supporting oral assessments and revising. For the purposes of this chapter let us consider how to use mind mapping for revision. The technique of mind mapping for revision is best learnt early on in the Key Stage 3 curriculum. At this stage the amount of information and the concepts within each topic are relatively simple. This allows the student to focus on the skill of learning how to mind map. It also teaches them that when you mind map there is no escape from the piece of information you need to know, but which you do not understand. With mind maps you cannot just skip over it. Often it becomes a habit to skip the parts of revision that are difficult and just hope they will not come up in the exam or test. (If you do this on a mind map an empty branch stares back at you reminding you to grapple with it.)

Students are often asked to revise for a test for homework, but they don't know how. They passively read their notes, perhaps over and over again. They may reduce their notes to shorter notes and yet still be unable to recall and link the vital key words. Mind mapping is active revision; it involves the student in a creative act and is hence memorable. To illustrate how to create a mind map I have used the Year 7 science topic 'Understanding living things'.

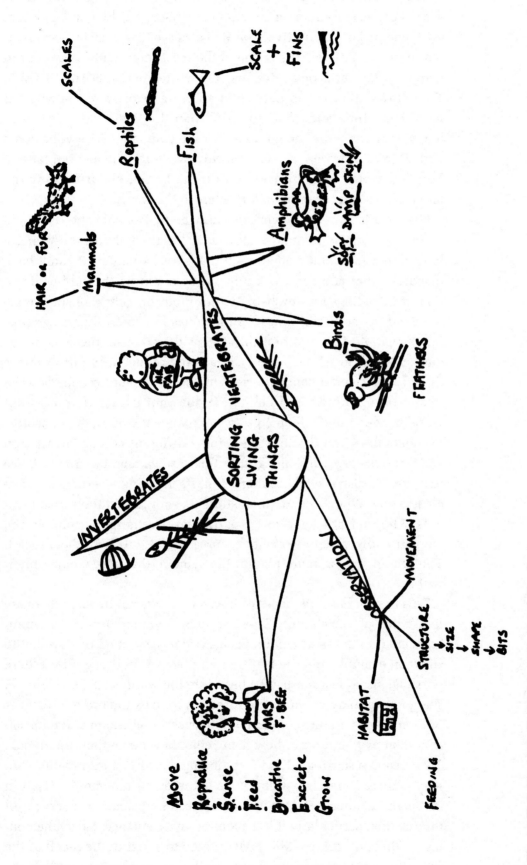

Figure 5.4 *Mind map for 'Understanding living things'*

First, the key concept is drawn in the centre of the page. It is best to use A3 paper, since mind maps should be big and bold, but the back of wallpaper is just as effective. You will also see that the words are written in capital letters. This is one of the most important rules of mind mapping. All words on a mind map are written in CAPITAL LETTERS. This draws attention to particular spelling features of the word. It takes more time and effort to write than the lower case word and hence remains more memorable. Try for yourself. Write your name and address in lower-case letters. Now write it using capital letters. You will feel your brain having to think harder about forming the letter shapes and the order of the letters in the word.

Next, students need to work out how many key concepts are going to be on their mind map. This will let them know how many branches to form and so help with the layout. Chapters 3 and 4 have discussed that you can work this out by counting the subheadings. Four subheadings will probably require four branches. In some texts there will be no subheadings; you may need to count the paragraphs. Six paragraphs in a text probably means there are six pieces of information to learn. Already the task is being reduced. In our example there are four main concepts: vertebrates; invertebrates; characteristics of living things; and habitat. It does not matter if you cannot work this out; they will emerge as you reduce the notes to key words. Students draw the first branch using a different colour felt-tip pen and write the key word along it, in this case vertebrates. You will see that there is also a symbol to represent its meaning – vertebrates have a backbone. Wherever possible, students should add their own symbols. They do not have to be particularly artistic; as long as the student knows what the symbol represents, it will help them recall. The funnier, ruder, more playful the symbol, the more memorable it will be.

This branch has five pieces of information within it, since there are five types of vertebrates. These branches extend from your main branch but in the same colour. Each word has a picture or a symbol to show an example and the feature that places it in this group. Where possible, visual features can be built into the word, such as in 'blood'. The pictures may be multi-coloured, as long as the branch remains predominantly in one colour. (Under stress in an exam students can shut their eyes and recall how many colours were on their mind map. This creates a starting point for retrieving the correct information.) So why is there a man in a T-shirt? He is there as a mnemonic. Used in moderation, mnemonics on mind maps can help some students recall information, particularly if it is required in a sequence. Save mnemonics for these occasions. MR. FAB is there to assist in the recall of the five categories: Mammals, Reptiles, Fish, Amphibians and Birds.

Fussy MRS BEG is there to assist in remembering the seven character-istics of living things.

Each branch is built in this manner until all of the information is recorded as in the completed mind map. You will notice that there are now very few words, and those that are there are important for recall, understanding and, where needed, spelling.

A word of caution

Many revision books now incorporate mind maps with the text. Although this at least begins to recognise that students have different learning styles, their main use is in active revision, with the students producing their own mindmaps. In my opinion, mindmaps are useless unless they are produced personally. As a teaching assistant you may be able to support students' first efforts by providing the framework of initial branches. In addition, some school departments have gone 'mind map mad'. A key thread through this book is that different students suit different techniques and mind mapping is not for every student. Ensure students try them once or twice before rejecting them, but if they do not work, do not insist on using them.

In summary, we all have differing memory capacities. Additionally, we all remember things in different ways. At present, to be successful within the education system, particularly with exams, students must be able to learn and recall facts as well as skills. Currently, we use very little of our brain's potential. Estimates range from 1 per cent to 2 per cent of its capacity. This means that by supporting students in utilis-ing a variety of techniques every student can improve their memory skills and manage their own memory more effectively.

End-of-chapter checklist (tick when achieved)

- ☐ I understand the difference between long- and short-term memory.

- ☐ I use familiar words to help students link new words correctly in their memory.

- ☐ I understand that some students' brains work more slowly and I must allow them time to think before I expect a response.

- ☐ I understand why I must discourage shouting out.

- ☐ I have a copy of all key topic words produced by subject departments.

- ☐ I have helped compile topic word lists by working with subject departments.

- ☐ I know what a mnemonic is.

- ☐ I have supported students by making some meaningful mnemonics.

- ☐ I have trialled the number peg system with a student.

- ☐ I have trialled the story method system with a student.

- ☐ I have supported students in making mind maps for revision.

- ☐ I have identified individual students and their preferred memory methods.

Supporting revision and exam skills

Chapter overview

Question: 'How do you eat an elephant?' Answer: 'A little at a time.'

Students find the prospect of exams daunting. This chapter is designed to help you support students who are preparing for and sitting exams. By the end of this chapter you will:

- understand the revision–recall–review continuum;
- learn how to plan a revision timetable;
- be able to recommend a variety of ways of revising for exams, suited to both the subject and the student's learning style;
- understand why exam nerves cause the brain to 'go blank';
- develop the skill of close reading, required for exam questions and instructions; and
- learn how to highlight and interpret key words in examination questions.

Understanding the revision–recall–review continuum

Picture yourself standing at one end of a large cornfield, the corn at full height. Now imagine you had to run through that field, from one side to the other. It would be quite hard work and time-consuming. You would have to make a pathway through, and by the time you had reached the other side, most of the pathway would have disappeared, as the corn would have sprung up again. However, if you ran through that field, taking the same route, every day for two weeks, gradually the pathway would be made. By the end of the two weeks it would be easy to run through, and would take much less time.

For students, preparing for examinations and undertaking revision is very much like this. Revision does not mean looking at each subject only once. The first time students revise a topic it is hard; they may have forgotten much of what they were taught. They may have lost some of the skills, and the time taken to process and remember everything that was taught seems long and daunting. Therefore, it is essential, when revising, that the material is worked with more than once. In that way, by the time the external exams arrive at the end of GSCEs, the materials and skills are very familiar, and the 'cornfield' is easy to 'run' through. This is why teachers have end-of-unit tests and end-of-year examinations. For example, once embarking on GCSE courses, students will have: end-of-unit tests; end-of-Year 10 exams; mock exams in Year 11; and then, finally, the external GCSE exam. This means several subject topics will have been revised and experience of the types of questions asked in exams will have been gained in a spiral of learning and relearning. If you can explain the reason why students should take each assessment seriously and use every opportunity to revise thoroughly for all of these, they will have much more chance of success. Otherwise they will be tempted to take school tests less seriously and not revise for them.

Using the revision–recall–review continuum

In order to gain the most from revision there are two important factors to recognise about how the brain learns and remembers: first, how we *recall* information we have learned; and second, how to understand the power of continuous *review* in order to ensure the material stays fresh in the mind (Buzan 1989).

Recall

During a learning period, which may be a taught lesson or a homework or revision session, we are most likely to remember what has been covered at the beginning and the end of the session. Experience shows we tend to find the middle of the sessions less memorable. People's concentration spans are also a lot smaller than you may think. The majority of us can concentrate for between 20 and 50 minutes, 20 minutes being more common in younger students at Key Stage 3.

Suppose a student has been revising for 50 minutes. They will probably remember the first 15 minutes and the last 15 minutes. This means they will forget approximately 20 minutes of the content covered in the middle of the session. Increasing the revision session to 1 hour 10 minutes is unlikely to increase the amount they remember, since it is difficult to concentrate for much longer. They will still probably remember the first 15 minutes or perhaps 20 minutes, and the last 15–20 minutes, but the amount forgotten in the middle has now increased to 30 minutes. You can see from the pie charts below that over the period of a week of revision this recall effect is quite dramatic.

This means that students must be trained to plan revision sessions in short bursts of approximately 30–50 minutes if they are to maximise its effect.

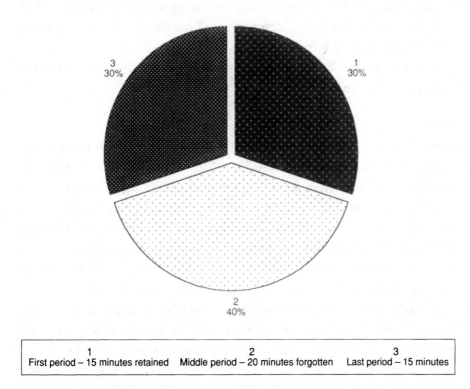

1	2	3
First period – 15 minutes retained	Middle period – 20 minutes forgotten	Last period – 15 minutes

Figure 6.1(a) *50-minute revision session*

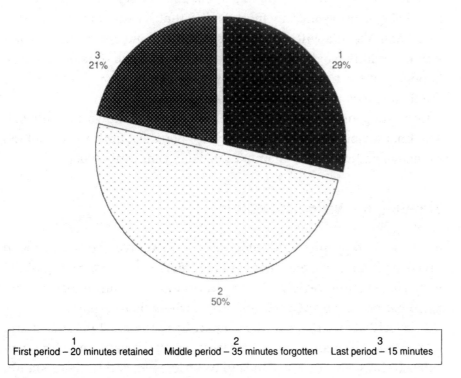

1	2	3
First period – 20 minutes retained	Middle period – 35 minutes forgotten	Last period – 15 minutes

Figure 6.1(b) *70-minute revision session*

Taking breaks

After 20 to 50 minutes students need to take a short break, and then change subject or topic before continuing. Breaks really must be breaks. They are not for parents to decide how they should be filled. For example, saying 'As you're not doing anything can you empty the dishwasher' is not a break!

These ideas will be returned to below when we look at designing a revision programme.

Review

How often have you been taught how to do something, for example a new skill on the computer, and then forgotten how to do it the next time you try? How often have you heard students say in frustration, 'I used to be able to do this'? The answer is probably 'very often'. This is quite normal. We all forget knowledge and skills unless we use them continuously. In particular, we need to practise a new skill straightaway. Revision is exactly the same; unless we continually review, go over, what we have revised it will not stay fresh in our mind.

The first time we learn something we are likely to remember about 20 per cent of it, if we do not review it. However, if we review it within 24 hours we can ensure we remember around 40 per cent. A further review one day later will ensure that we remember even more. Adding to this review, two days later, and then a further review one week later, will ensure even more is recalled. Some experts will tell you that this will ensure you remember 100 per cent. However, as we noted above, everyone's memory is different. I cannot guarantee that reviewing like this will ensure the student remembers everything, but it will certainly maximise what they can recall. Each time the material is reviewed the time taken for the review can be shortened, until by the final review it is just a five-minute glance.

Good revision for one topic may look like that shown in Table 6.1. The final review could be repeated once per week until the day of the exam, depending on the amount of revision time available.

Planning a revision timetable

For many end-of-unit tests students will only have enough notice to revise perhaps once, and then add one review on the morning of the test. This section deals with preparation and planning for external examinations, such as GCSEs and SATs, where there is more time.

It is unlikely that any student, apart from the most organised and motivated, will manage to cover every aspect of every topic for every subject. However, any revision is to be welcomed, and students should

Table 6.1 Revision–review plan for the subject of geography (topic: volcanoes)

date	Topic	Revision method	Time spent	Amount remembered
02.05.04	GCSE Volcanoes, causes, types and effects plus case study	Make mind map using notes in exercise book and textbook	50 minutes	20–30%
03.05.04	Volcanoes, causes, types and effects plus case study	Check mind map, draw rough copy from memory. Add colour, pictures etc. to key words forgotten	15 minutes	40–50%
04.05.04	Volcanoes, causes, types and effects plus case study	Check mind map, try exam question in note form, from study book, revision website or past paper	10 minutes	60%
06.05 05	Volcanoes, causes, types and effects plus case study	Glance over mind map, think of one or two questions I could be asked.	5 minutes	70–80%
13.05.05	Volcanoes, causes, types and effects plus case study	Glance over mind map, check everything is retained and understood	5 minutes	80%+

not worry about the entire 'elephant' but start to feel secure in tackling the revision a little at a time.

Filling in a weekly revision planner is essential and must be stuck to rigorously. Below is a guide to filling in a weekly revision planner, a blank copy of which can be found in appendix 6.1.

1. **Get organised:** Before filling in the weekly planner students need to compile a list of the topics that must be revised for each subject. Where necessary, help them to separate the topics out into lists that represent the separate exams within that subject. For example, the maths topic lists can be separated into calculator paper and non-calculator paper. It is amazing how many students do not know the exam board for their individual subjects and do not make themselves aware of each syllabus. This is despite the fact that many teachers get them to write this at the beginning of their GCSE course. Revision is a useful time to re-focus students on this, together with the length of each exam and the amount of marks it is worth as a proportion of the whole GCSE. Most teachers will give

students lists of the topics that need to be revised. Lists can also be found in the exam syllabus and published revision guides. Being proactive as a teaching assistant and collecting subjects' topic lists in advance can also be useful. One section of the chemistry list for GCSE double Science may look like this:

Earth materials:
- Crude oil
- Fractional distillation
- Hydrocarbons – using and cracking
- Alkanes and alkenes
- Polymers and plastics
- Extracting iron – the blast furnace
- Uses of 3 common metals
- 4 Uses of limestone
- Ammonia – making (the Haber Process) and using as fertiliser

If possible, colour-code the lists. All chemistry lists could be written on yellow paper. Make sure the lists are placed in a folder; piles of loose paper all over the place will only lead to feeling overwhelmed by the size of the task. Use post-it stickers or subject dividers to separate out subjects in revision folders. It is at this point that students can feel overwhelmed as they look at the huge amount that has to be revised. Try to reassure them that as long as they plan ahead and tackle each one at a time it will be manageable.

2. **Put onto the weekly planner all commitments and social activities.** This is where students need to be really honest. If they watch every episode of *East Enders*, including the omnibus on Sundays, this needs to go onto the planner first. A revision timetable can only be adhered to if it is realistic. If they don't get up until 2.00 p.m. on a Sunday it is pointless filling in a Sunday morning revision slot.

3. **Begin to fill in the slots:** morning, afternoon and evening revision slots. Each revision slot must:

- be no more than 50 minutes long;
- include short breaks in between;
- include the *subject* and then the selected *topic* within the subject and the *method of revision*. This is very important; by writing the actual topic and the method of revision the temptation to procrastinate is resisted;
- include *review periods* for topics revised on previous days and weeks to ensure that recall is as high as possible;
- Include, over the day and week, a balance of subjects, with different revision methods so that the student stays fresh and does not avoid the subjects or topics they do not like.

Making thorough weekly revision timetables is the sure way to exam success.

Below is an example of a completed revision planner for one week, from a student who is an 'early bird' and does not work well late in the evenings.

Revision methods and styles

'I never know how to revise English, so I just don't revise it.' This is a comment I heard very recently from a motivated student embarking on her GCSE course.

Different subjects lend themselves to differing revision methods, as well as individual students having preferred learning styles. In addition, due to differing learning styles, students need to experiment with their study environment:

- where they complete their revision: some students work best on the floor in their own bedroom; others like to be in the family kitchen where they don't feel cut off;

- when their recall is best: do they remember more if they work in the morning, or do they prefer working late into the evening?

- with their preferred learning environment: do they work better with music on, or do they require complete silence? How warm or cold do they like the room to be? Do they prefer very bright light or quite dull light?

   All of these environmental preferences will affect the recall of their revision. Some students even use different perfumes or scented candles when they revise different subjects, in order to have a further sensory link for their memory.

Suggested revision methods (a copy is in Appendix 6.2 to share with students)

1. Make summary notes using A4 paper or file cards; colour code the notes.

2. Make patterned notes or mind maps; stick the mind maps all over the bedroom, loo walls etc. for quick reviews.

3. Change headings into questions and write summary notes that answer those questions.

4. Compare your summary notes to friends' notes and shop-bought revision notes.

5. Read your summary notes aloud, put them onto tape and listen to them in the car for quick reviews.

Table 6.2 Weekly Planner – revision and review chart week 1

Day	Sunday	Monday	Tuesday	Wednesday	Thursday	Friday	Saturday
Morning Session 1 (50 mins) Session 2 (50 mins) Session 3 (30 mins)	Geography – Volcanoes – mind map Finish mind map English – poetry choose 2 poems and re read + notes	Review Geog mind map – re-do bits if needed. Human – geog settlement make notes from ex. bk +revision guide D.T. Make list of all technical vocab-learn Maths-algebra text bk	English – check I know alliteration, similes etc. find examples in poems. Chemistry – Fractional distillation label chart. Go on BBC Revisewise for chem. And maths simultaneous eq – top-up algebra	Biology top-up cells revision – draw cells from memory check name and job of each cell. Mind map of photo synthesis French family and friends for oral, reading and writing, make cards with pics.	Do physics question on light on my own. Revision bk. Mind map on sound waves Write character descriptions and themes of novel Go swimming	French – check family and friends. Write letter to pen friend with info in, check vocab correct. Add house and home, use post-it notes round house. (Pink la blue le) R.E. Plan essay on World religions – Judaism	Lie in Do English persuasive letter under timed conditions – stick to plan
LUNCH							
Afternoon Session 1 (50 mins) Session 2 (50 mins) Session 3 (30 mins)	French – practise vocab – all about me – do questions and answers on to tape East Enders Omnibus	Meet Jenny, revise French oral together from yesterday. Jenny to do physics 'light' for me – me to do maths simultaneous equations	Afternoon off, shopping with Jenny	Top up settlement, see if notes have worked. Go to D.T. revision class run by dept. Ask English teacher to check essay plans from last week.	Top up photosynthesis formula check on Revision website and past question Maths – volume text book questions Start R.E revision, make topic list	Chemistry top-up distillation, add alkenes and alkanes make mnemonic cos. get confused. Learn 2 physics formulas Essay plan on persuasive letter writing, make one up	Geog top-up volcanoes and settlements – brain storm and post-it notes – check still in! Start Tectonic plates and earth quakes – watch the video Visit Nan
TEA							
Evening 1 Session 50 mins	Biology – cells draw and label cells Make mind map of specialised cells	Maths – Fractions Use textbook 8.00-8.30 p.m.watch East Enders finish	Answer question on volcanoes in my head Listen to English novel on tape in bed	Watch East Enders	Answer exam questions on photosynthesis, Biology revision guide. Watch East Enders Listen to novel on tape	Night out with friends no revision (Tape East Enders)	Jenny coming round to revise, teach her algebra – brackets and factorising, Jenny teach me how to balance equations in Chem. French – test each other French vocab so far. Watch DVD

6. Get others to read your summary notes aloud to you.

7. Rewrite your summary notes using different words and layout.

8. Practise labelling diagrams without looking at your notes; make sure you can spell the key words.

9. Test yourself using 'read, cover up, write and check'.

10. Test yourself by visualising; draw the picture or movie in your mind. This method works for Olympic athletes so it will work for you.

11. Get others to test you, answer verbally or write it down.

12. Be active when testing yourself; move around the room.

13. Do past exam papers, first using your notes, then without using your notes.

14. Do past exam papers under timed conditions.

15. Do lots of plans of English essays from past papers; ask your teacher to check your plan is suitable for the essay title.

16. Work through examples from textbooks; cover up as you go along and continue to self-check.

17. Think up your own exam questions. This is really hard but shows that you know the topic.

18. Be metacognitive at all times (know the number of facts to recall, the number of key words etc.).

19. Share the revision with a friend; take a topic each, revise it thoroughly and teach it to one another. Share with a friend who is better at a subject than you are, and who is less secure with another subject than you are. Supporting each other in this way raises your self-esteem.

20. Form a revision group with friends. You will chat a little to start with, but then you will settle down.

21. Remember to review your learning; think of the recall–review continuum.

22. Take lots of breaks.

23. Exercise during revision times; this increases the oxygen to your brain, relieves stress and makes you tired so that you sleep well.

24. Use post-it notes on your walls, cupboards etc.

25. Use post-it notes with the French/German/Spanish nouns and verbs on and stick them on as many household and school objects you are allowed to.

26. Collect all of the post-it notes and see how quickly you can run round the house or classroom replacing them.

27. Use travel time in the car, bus etc. to listen to revision tapes, either bought ones or your own. In particular, buy tapes of unabridged versions of novels to help you picture the characters and settings as you listen.

28. Make up rhymes and mnemonics for facts that must be recalled in the correct sequence.

29. Make up stories to remember the key words for essay plans.

30. Use all of your senses to aid your memory.

31. Use television programmes to relate your learning to real life. With all of the channels available now most geography and history topics are covered in some way.

32. Watch/listen to the news; it may relate to your modern language knowledge, science, history, geography, English and maths.

33. Read novels that give backgrounds that support historical and geographical knowledge.

34. Tackle difficult revision when you are fresh.

35. Video-record revision programmes, such as *GCSE Bite Size*, so that you can time-shift.

36. Use the revision sites available; most schools are now linked to these sites and can give you your own password so that you can access them at home.

37. Use PowerPoint on your PC for preparation of orals in Modern Foreign Language exams.

38. Select the appropriate methods of revision for the topic involved. Maths does not lend itself to mind mapping; it is better to use the maths textbook for worked examples and revision exercises, and then past papers.

39. Keep metacognitve at all times about what methods are working for you, in which subjects and at what time of day you seem to recall best.

Exam skills

Good preparation, in the form of well-planned revision and review, will prepare all students for their actual exams. However, there are additional skills that are required during examinations in order to ensure that all of that time and commitment in the preparation stage pays dividends.

Exam nerves and human nature

In preparation for an extended examination period – for example the Key Stage 3 SATs or the longer period of GCSEs – students often find it useful to understand how their brain works. If you are aware of this you can explain it to them and its practical implications.

The brain is sometimes referred to as the 'triune' brain; that is it has three layers. This term was proposed by neurologist Paul Maclean. If you wish to read about this in detail a search on the internet using 'triune brain' or 'P. Maclean' will give more information. The first layer is the oldest part of the brain; the reptilian brain. This part concerns itself with basic functions, such as ensuring we have water when we are thirsty, and are not too cold or too hot. The second layer is called the 'limbic' brain. This controls emotions. Finally, the largest part of the brain, and the newest part in terms of human evolution, is the neo-cortex, or thinking brain. This is the part we want to be working at full power during the exam.

So why is it necessary to understand this in order to improve exam success? Think of the layers in terms of a *hierarchy* (Chapter 3), the lowest part needing to be satisfied first before the next part can work efficiently. The reptilian brain needs to be satisfied first. After all, in

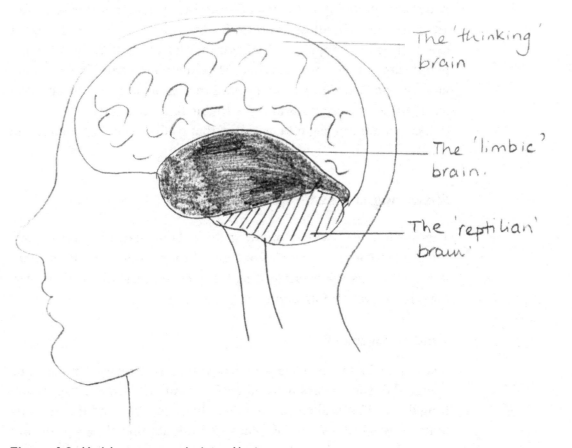

Figure 6.2 *Model to represent the 'triune' brain*

terms of survival, basic needs are the most necessary. This means suggesting to students that they have eaten (particularly breakfast), had enough sleep and that they are not too hot or cold before they go into the exam. Secondly, the limbic brain needs to feel secure and safe in order to work effectively. Therefore, having an argument with mum or a friend just before an exam is not a good idea. Additionally, students often have conversations outside the exam hall about their revision, the exam format or the equipment they have or have not got. These can sometimes be unsettling, indeed some students delight in unsettling other students as they wait. Therefore, as a teaching assistant you need to advise them not to do this. By all means check they have all of the necessary equipment, but encourage them to talk about enjoyable experiences and topics that relax them rather than the exam itself. This will allow the limbic brain to feel settled.

Once inside the exam room, students will feel the full effect of their limbic brain. As the papers are handed out their hearts will race, their hands may feel sweaty and they may feel sick. The effect of this is to shut down the thinking brain until the limbic system settles. This is the dreaded 'going blank' that some students experience. But if students understand that what is happening is natural they can use relaxation techniques, give themselves time to settle, read through the paper and gradually convince their limbic system that it is safe after all. This will then allow the thinking brain to work efficiently. Most exam disasters happen at the beginning of the GCSE period when people are at their most nervous. Many careless errors in exams are made at the beginning of the exam. Finally, once the reptilian brain has fulfilled its functions and the limbic brain has settled down, the thinking brain can begin to use all of that well-revised knowledge and skills.

Answering the exam question

This section deals with supporting students in answering exam questions effectively. Successful exam technique involves three main factors: time management; reading the question carefully; and answering with *relevant* information.

Time management

Just as time had to be managed effectively during revision it has to be managed during the exam. The first five minutes need to be spent settling down. This will allow the limbic brain to settle and the thinking brain to work at its best. Explain to students that they should not worry if they see others starting to write immediately. This is not good exam practice. They need to settle and read the instructions of the exam carefully, which you will hear referred to as the exam *rubrics*. This will ensure they answer questions from the correct sections of the paper and read the advice as to how long to spend on each section.

Students often think that the time allocated to an exam is all for writing. You need to explain that there is time built into each exam for reading, thinking, writing and checking their answers. In addition, students work at different speeds, their thinking speed (discussed as 'processing speed' in Chapter 5), their reading speed and their writing speed. When examiners set exam papers they select an optimum time allowance for each exam, but it would be odd if every student had exactly the correct amount of time; some will finish early, some will finish exactly on time, and others because they time-managed meticulously. Students need to appreciate this and relate their time management to their own working speed. The main factor is to keep an eye on the time throughout the exam so that all questions are attempted. It is no good completing one essay out of three excellently and not having time to complete the other two. (This is also the time to point out to students the value of writing essay plans *within* the exam. If they do run out of time on the last question, at least the examiner can look at their plan and give some marks for what they were going to do.) Similarly, it is useless struggling with one maths question for so long that they do not have time to attempt others that they may be able to do quickly and easily.

Reading the question carefully

This is probably the biggest area in which most students' skills are deficient. However, this skill can and must be practised alongside revision when looking at past papers. You can also put this into practice every time you listen to a student read out a question from a textbook or test during normal classroom activities. The different types of reading strategies are discussed in Chapter 3. Exam reading requires a particular type of reading, known as *close reading*. In close reading you must slow down and read word for word exactly what is there. Here is a list of common reading errors and 'do nots' to help with close reading skills:

<u>Do not</u> substitute simple words like 'a' for 'the'. 'Give *the* reason for your answer' suggests there is only one possible reason you can give. Give '*a*' reason for your answer suggests there are several possible answers for you to choose from.

<u>Do not</u> omit the 's' off the ends of words, or add one if it is not there. 'Give reasons for your answer' means you are expected to give more than one.

<u>Do not</u> turn a positive into a negative, or a negative into a positive. 'Why does the poet . . .' is very different from 'Why doesn't the poet . . .'.

<u>Do not</u> skip words, by slipping back into skimming skills. Close reading works best when you use your finger and move it along the question as you read each individual word to yourself.

<u>Do not</u> misread two words that look visually similar if read quickly, for example 'reflect' and 'rotate', 'Saturday' for 'Sunday' on timetable charts in maths exams.

So what are close reading skills? First, they are *different* reading skills; you only need to use them occasionally, exams being one example.

Here is a list of DOs for close reading.

<u>Do</u> slow down, especially if you know you are a fast, careless reader by nature.

<u>Do</u> read the question more than once.

<u>Do</u> use a highlighter pen to highlight all of the *key words* in the question. This is an essential piece of equipment for students in all exams. They must get used to using this skill; without it they will make mistakes. Most exams questions have a verb instruction, i.e. '*write* down', '*choose* one example', '*explain*'. In addition many exam questions use the six W words discussed in Chapters 3 and 4, i.e. '*how* did', '*why* did', etc. All 'W' words need to be highlighted in exam questions. Students need practice in recognising and understanding how to respond to many of the exam words such as:

Compare and contrast

Describe in detail

Explain

Evaluate

Calculate

Simplify

Show how

Sum up (very different meaning in English exams to maths exams)

<u>Do</u> make use of the *italics* and **bold** words in the question. They have been put there to support the student.

<u>Do</u> ensure students recognise the subtle change in meaning of words in different subject areas. For example, 'Illustrate your answer' means give an example, or case study, in most exam subjects, but lots of students draw a picture! Factors in maths are different from factors in history: 'Calculate the angle' means work out, whereas 'Measure the angle' means use your protractor!

Figure 6.3

Look at the exam question below:

'Explain how the structure of the human heart is adapted to a double circulatory system.'

What words would you highlight in this question?
  Look at the student's response:

The human heart has a double circulatory system; it is adapted this way so that blood can be taken to the lungs quicker. We can do various exercises better this way because of the double circulatory system. Oxygenated blood can be taken to the lungs and around the body twice as fast.

The student scored 0 out of the 4 marks available. It is clear that he/she understands the double circulatory system, but they have discussed *why* humans have a double circulatory system; the question asked to explain *how* the *structure* is *adapted*. Therefore, key words connected to 'structure' were required, such as the two pumps and four chambers of the heart, the valves and the function of the left half and the right half. These key words would have gained marks.

Answering the question and keeping on answering the question

We have already discussed the need to ensure that the question has been read carefully and understood. Surely this should now be enough to ensure that the question is answered. However, good exam technique means being able to select from acquired knowledge carefully and use only *relevant* information. The amount of information required will depend upon the title of the question and the amount of marks available. Students need to keep referring back to the original question, their highlighting and their plan to ensure that they are still answering it and have not wandered off into irrelevant areas. Often students are very tempted, particularly having revised a subject thoroughly, to give the examiner everything they know about a topic. But it is not the examiner's job to wade through the answer and find the relevant parts; it is the student's job to make the answer relevant. In addition, writing unnecessary information is a waste of time and will impact on the amount of time left for other relevant answers. Finally, examiners recognise a padded-out answer when they see one.

As a teaching assistant you could not emphasise enough the need to keep checking back to the original question to ensure it is still being answered. In maths, which often requires a sequence of operations, this will ensure that a student does not get half way through and think they have finished the question. In English this will ensure that they use all of the guidelines in the question and discuss all of the bullet points needed for a full answer; for example, the author's use of language, the way the characters behave and how the characters feel. In history this will ensure that they only select relevant facts and opinions to discuss in relation to the sources.

Walking away

As a footnote, you need to encourage students to walk away after an exam and not discuss it with their peers. Once the paper has been handed in there is nothing they can do. Having a post mortem afterwards does no good. If it was disaster it needs to be put aside so that preparation for the next exam can take place with a relaxed mind. If it went well, they can quietly analyse why, and transfer those skills to the next exam.

Summary

Taking exams is stressful for all students; but no student, whatever their ability, wishes to leave school without the qualifications that demonstrate what they have learned over 11 years. This chapter has described revision and examination methods that will enable you to support students in preparing appropriately, and maximising their success.

End-of-chapter checklist (tick when achieved)

- ☐ I understand how students recall information over time.

- ☐ I understand the importance of review.

- ☐ I have helped plan a student revision timetable.

- ☐ I have collated together topic lists working with different subject departments.

- ☐ I am aware of a variety of different revision methods to suggest to students, which suit both the subject and their preferred learning style.

- ☐ I could describe the triune brain to a student and explain its importance in exams.

- ☐ I know what rubrics are and can explain their importance to students.

- ☐ I can explain how to close read for exam questions and practise this skill with students in class when they are reading questions aloud to me.

- ☐ I model, using a highlighter pen, wherever possible to highlight key words in questions. I encourage students to highlight key words.

- ☐ I discuss the meaning of exam words to ensure students are clear about their specific meanings.

- ☐ I use feedback from tests and homework to explain the importance of re-reading questions and using relevant information.

- ☐ I encourage students to use key words from their revision in exam answers.

Appendix 1.1: VAK metaphors

Auditory learners

I hear where you are coming from.
That rings a bell.
It's music to my ears.
He's talking rubbish.
She's drummed that into me.
I like your story.
We're on the same wavelength.
We sing from the same hymn-sheet.
Quiet as a mouse.
A ding-dong row.
That gives me a buzz.
I'm lost for words.
I hear you loud and clear.
Tell me what you mean.

Kinaesthetic learners

Show me what you mean.
Do it like this.
I'm ready to tackle this.
One step at a time.
I've got a good feeling about this.
You hit the nail on the head.
Get a grip of yourself.
This is a sticky situation.
Give me something concrete to go on.
Her feelings were hurt.
Hold on a minute.
I can feel it in my bones.

> **Add you own observations and decide if they are V, A or K.**

Visual learners

I see what you mean.
Try to see it my way.
Things are looking up.
He makes me see red.
It's one of my most vivid memories.
That sheds light on the matter.
That's crystal clear.
Look on the bright side.
I can see right though her.
We see eye to eye.
He turns a blind eye.
It appears that…

Appendix 1.2: Visually learning the times table

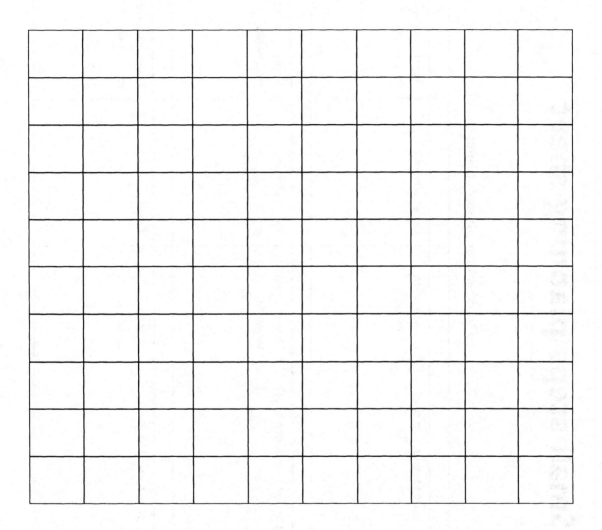

Suggested order: ×1, ×10, ×5, ×9 (produced visually), ×2, ×3, ×4, ×6, ×7, ×8

Time taken:

Error rate:

Appendix 2.1: Small steps planning sheet

Target to be reached:

Number of small steps planned:

Small step			
	What am I going to do to reach step one?	Date to reach target by:	Target achieved	Target maintained for 2 weeks

Small step			
	What am I going to do to reach step one?	Date to reach target by:	Target achieved	Target maintained for 2 weeks

Small step			
	What am I going to do to reach step one?	Date to reach target by:	Target achieved	Target maintained for 2 weeks

Appendix 3.1: Hierarchy of questions

Lowest level to highest level

Literal comprehension

The information needed to respond to the question is within the passage. The text does not need to be rearranged and the answers can be lifted from the text. This simple task can be made more complex by changing the vocabulary of the question.

Comprehension reorganisation

This consists of adjusting information to respond to the question. The information is still within the text. The type of tasks here could involve taking facts from a passage and writing the facts again in your own words.

Inferential comprehension

This consists of looking at the implications of the reading. The reader must use the information in the passage and add to that his or her experiences in order to respond to the question. This is the type of question when you begin to say to yourself, 'But it doesn't say!'. It means reading between the lines.

Evaluation

Quite high levels of thinking are required. The reader must make judgements and compare criteria in the passage with external criteria. They must be aware of bias, purpose and audience. The responses could include:

Could this really have happened?
Was this right or wrong?
What do you think of the passage? (Personal response)

Appreciation

The highest level of thinking; getting to grips with what the writer had in mind when writing the story or information. Being aware of the resonance of the text and the text genre. It requires use of imagery, sensory ideas and abstract thought.

Questions for the hierarchy of comprehension skills

Knowledge level

- What happened after...?
- How many...?
- Who was it...?
- Describe what happened...
- Who spoke to...?
- Can you tell me who...?
- Find the meaning of...
- What is...?
- Is this true or false...?

Literal comprehension level

- Can you tell me in your own words about this?
- Write a short summary
- What do you think could have happened next?
- Find the main idea in this text
- Who was the main character?
- Can you distinguish between?
- What differences exist between?
- Give an example of what you mean by...
- If someone asked you what this meant could you give them a definition?

Comprehension level (inferential)

- Do you know another example where...?
- Could this really have happened?
- What ideas would you change if...?
- Can you transfer the method used to another subject?
- Do you recognise this from an experience that you have had?
- How is this information useful to you?

Evaluation level

- Which event could not have happened?
- Identify the underlying themes of this novel
- What are some of the problems with this information?
- What was the turning point in the story?
- What was the problem with...?
- What was the author's intention?
- What is the intended audience for this?
- Can you design a...to...?
- What is a possible solution to this problem?
- How many ways can you...?
- Can you create new and unusual uses for...?
- Is there a better solution to...?
- Judge the value of...?
- Do you think... is a good or a bad thing? Explain.
- What sort of a character is this?
- What do you think about...?
- How effective are/is...?
- Do you agree with...? How would you justify your opinion?
- Is this a fair test?

Appendix 4.1: 'Purpose, audience, structure' reminder sheet

All good writing needs to start with a 'pas'.

This stands for:

purpose: What is the piece of writing for?

audience: Who am I writing this for?

structure: Having answered the two questions above now what **Structure** is suitable for my writing at the word, sentence and text level?

Appendix 4.2: The six Ws writing frame

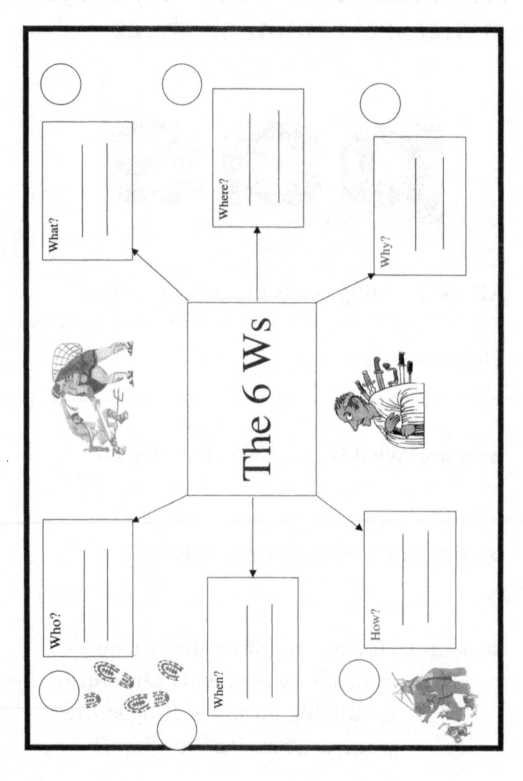

Appendix 4.3: Constructing a balanced written argument writing frame

Arguments against...

MINUS points

Arguments for...

PLUS points

Useful connective words and phrases for linking writing in the passive tense. Firstly, secondly, finally, besides, moreover, however, furthermore, too, also, as well, nevertheless

- Several people think that...
- Many people believe that...
- It is, however, possible that...
- It is often (sometimes) said that...
- In spite of this...

Constructing a balanced written argument

My personal opinion

Appendix 6.1: Weekly planner: revision and review chart

	Sunday	Monday	Tuesday	Wednesday	Thursday	Friday	Saturday
Morning							
Afternoon							
Evening							

Appendix 6.2: Suggested revision methods

1. Make summary notes using A4 paper or file cards; colour code the notes.
2. Make patterned notes or mind maps; stick the mind maps all over the bedroom, loo walls etc. for quick reviews.
3. Change headings into questions and write summary notes that answer those questions.
4. Compare your summary notes to friends' notes and shop-bought revision notes.
5. Read your summary notes aloud, put them onto tapes and listen to them in the car for quick reviews.
6. Get others to read your summary notes aloud to you.
7. Rewrite your summary notes using different words and layout.
8. Practise labelling diagrams without looking at your notes; make sure you can spell the key words.
9. Test yourself using 'read, cover up, write and check'.
10. Test yourself by visualising, draw the picture or movie in your mind. This method works for Olympic athletes so it will work for you.
11. Get others to test you, answer verbally or write it down.
12. Be active when testing yourself; move around the room.
13. Do past exam papers, first *using* your notes, then *without* using your notes.
14. Do past exam papers under timed conditions.
15. Do lots of plans of English essays from past papers; ask your teacher to check your plan is suitable for the essay title.
16. Work through examples from textbooks; cover up as you go along and continue to self-check.
17. Think up your own exam questions. This is really hard but shows that you know the topic.
18. Be metacognitive at all times (know the number of facts to recall, the number of key words etc.).
19. Share the revision with a friend; take a topic each, revise it thoroughly and teach it to one another. Share with a friend who is better at a subject than you are and who is less secure with another subject than you are. Supporting each other in this way raises your self-esteem.
20. Form a revision group with friends. You will chat a little to start with, but then you will settle down.

21. Remember to review your learning; think of the recall–review continuum.
22. Take lots of breaks.
23. Exercise during revision times; this increases the oxygen to your brain, relieves stress and makes you tired so that you sleep well.
24. Use post-it notes on your walls, cupboards etc.
25. Use post-it notes with the French/German/Spanish nouns and verbs on and stick them on as many household and school objects you are allowed to.
26. Collect all of the post-it notes and see how quickly you can run round the house or classroom replacing them.
27. Use travel time in the car, bus etc. to listen to revision tapes, either bought ones or your own. In particular, buy tapes of unabridged versions of novels to help you picture the characters and settings as you listen.
28. Make up rhymes and mnemonics for facts that must be recalled in the correct sequence.
29. Make up stories to remember the key words for essay plans.
30. Use all of your senses to aid your memory.
31. Use television programmes to relate your learning to real life. With all of the channels available now most geography and history topics are covered in some way.
32. Watch/listen to the news; it may relate to your modern language knowledge, science, history, geography, English and maths.
33. Read novels that give backgrounds that support historical and geographical knowledge.
34. Tackle difficult revision when you are fresh.
35. Video-record revision programmes, such as *GCSE Bite Size* so that you can time-shift.
36. Use the revision sites available; most schools are now linked to these sites and can give you your own password so that you can access them at home.
37. Use PowerPoint on your PC for preparation of orals in Modern Foreign Language exams.
38. Select the appropriate methods of revision for the topic involved. Maths does not lend itself to mind mapping; it is better to use the maths textbook for worked examples and revision exercises, and then past papers.
39. Keep metacognitve at all times about what methods are working for you, in which subjects and at what time of day you seem to recall best.

Glossary

active learning	Learning that involves 'doing something' with the information, e.g. highlighting
auditory learners	Learning strength is by hearing and language
authorial skills	The skill of the writer to match the writing style to the type of text well
close reading	Slow, deliberate reading word by word, to ensure absolute accuracy
closed questions	A question that can have a one-word answer, usually 'yes' or 'no'
delayed gratification	Being able to put off gain until a later date while focusing on what needs to be done to achieve it.
emotive vocabulary	Words used to rouse feelings
genre	Writing that has specific features relating to its writing type, e.g. detective novel
hierarchy	A system in which things are put into an order from top to bottom
homophones	Words that sound the same but are spelt differently, e.g. 'there', 'their'
hook	A method of improving memory, i.e. attaching new word meaning to an already familiar word
information text	Written to enable the reader to know how to do something, e.g. a fire notice
irrelevant	Information that is not necessary or relevant to the topic being discussed
key words	Important words that carry the central meaning of the sentence or paragraph
kinaesthetic learners	Learning strength is by doing (motor skills)
metacognition	Thinking about how you did your thinking
mnemonic	A rhyme, word or phrase using the first letter of each word to help recall something, e.g. Richard of York gave battle in vain for the colours of the rainbow
models	A representation designed to show or describe something clearly
Neurolinguistic programming (NLP)	A method of looking at human interaction
on-line	linked to the World Wide Web (www)
open question	A question that requires more thought than a one-word answer
persuasive texts	Written to try to get the reader to agree with the writer's viewpoint
power sentence	The first key sentence in a paragraph, designed to guide the reader
recall	Similar to 'retrieve' (the prefix 're-' meaning 'again'). The ability to remember something
retained	To be able to keep something that has been learned
retrieve	To get back (from the memory)
rubric	Exam instructions
scanning	Looking for something specific within a text – numbers, names, key words
search engine	A means of trawling all sites on the Web, to index and categorise them to allow you to find something quickly
secretarial skills	The writing skills of correct grammar, punctuation, spelling and handwriting
skimming	A method of quick reading to get an initial overview
temporal awareness	An awareness of time and space
transfer	To be able to move a skill from one area to another
VAK	The Visual, Auditory and Kinaesthetic model of learning, used in multisensory teaching
visual learners	Learning strength is by sight, shape and colour
working memory	Involves the short-term memory in remembering and manipulating information

References

Almond, D. (1998) *Skellig*. London: Hodder Children's Books.

Buzan, T. (1989) *Use Your Head*. London: BBC Books.

Chinn, S. and Ashcroft, J. (1998) *Mathematics for Dyslexics: A Teaching Handbook* (2nd edn). London: Whurr.

DfEE (2001a) *Key Stage 3: The National Strategy Framework for Teaching English*. London: DfEE.

DfEE (2001b) *Literacy Across the Curriculum*. London: DfEE.

Gardner, H. (1983) *Frames of Mind*. New York: Basic Books.

Lewis, M. and Wray, D. (1998) *Writing Across the Curriculum: Frames to Support Learning*. Reading: Reading and Language Information Centre, University of Reading.

Lingard, J. (2000) *Natasha's' Will*. London: Penguin.

Oxford Interactive Encyclopaedia (1997) London: The Learning Company Inc.

www.geography.learnontheinternet.co.uk/topics/volcanoes

www.folkestonegirls.kent.sch.uk (accessed 17.05.04)

Additional reading

Buzan, T. (2003) *Mind Maps for Kids*. London: Thorsons.

Given, B.K. and Reid,G. (1999) *Learning Styles: A Guide for Teachers and Parents*. St Annes on Sea: Rose Publications.

Shaw, S. and Hawes, T. (1998) *Effective Teaching and Learning in the Primary Classroom*. Leicester: Optimal Learning.

Index

After a page number, an 'f.' or 't.' indicates inclusion of a figure or table; an 'a.' indicates an appendix.

Lightning Source UK Ltd.
Milton Keynes UK
UKOW040338241211

184344UK00002B/2/P